The Ethics of Management

The Ethics of Management

LARUE TONE HOSMER
Graduate School of Business Administration
University of Michigan

Second Edition

IRWIN
Homewood, IL 60430
Boston, MA 02116

Associate publisher: Martin F. Hanifin
Project editor: Paula M. Buschman
Production manager: Carma W. Fazio
Cover designer: David T. Jones
Compositor: Eastern Graphics
Typeface: 11/13 Baskerville
Printer: Arcata Graphics/Kingsport

Library of Congress Cataloging-in-Publication Data

Hosmer, LaRue T.
    The ethics of management / LaRue Tone Hosmer.—2nd ed.
        p.   cm.
    Includes bibliographical references and index.
    ISBN 0-256-08489-0
    1. Business ethics.   2. Industrial management—Moral and ethical
aspects.   I. Title.
HF5387.H67   1990
174'.4—dc20   90–45093

Printed in the United States of America
2 3 4 5 6 7 8 9 0 K 7 6 5 4 3 2 1

Preface

What is "right" and "proper" and "just"? These terms, and that question, are going to become more important in the future than in the past as our society becomes more crowded, our economy more competitive, and our technology more complex. These terms and that question are going to become particularly important for the business executive, whose decisions can affect so many people in ways that are outside of their own control.

The ethics of management—the determination of what is "right" and "proper" and "just" in the decisions and actions that affect other people—goes far beyond simple questions of bribery, theft and collusion. It focuses on what our relationships are—and ought to be—with our employees, our customers, our stockholders, our creditors, our suppliers, our distributors and our neighbors—members of the communities in which we operate. What do we owe to an employee who has been with the company for 28 years, yet now is no longer needed? What do we owe to a customer who purchased one of our mechanical products three years ago, yet now we realize that it may fail in operation and cause that person great inconvenience and perhaps some loss of safety? What do we owe to a distributor who helped us establish a major product line years ago, yet now represents an inefficient means of reaching the market? What do we owe to our stockholders, and how do we balance our duties to our stockholders with our obligations to these other groups?

This is the most critical issue in the ethics of management: the continual conflict between the economic performance of the firm, measured by revenues, costs and profits and owed to the stockholders, and the social performance of the firm, much more difficult to measure, but represented by obligations to employees, customers, creditors, suppliers, distributors, and members of the general public. If we discharge our employee who has 28 years of service but is no longer needed, our costs will go down, yet his life may be ruined. If we don't tell our customer about the design flaw in our product, our warranty expenses will be lower, yet she may be seriously inconvenienced and perhaps even hurt. If we replace our distributor by shipping directly from the factory to the retailers, our profits will increase, yet we may force that company out of business.

How do we decide when we face these issues? How do we determine what is "right" and "proper" amd "just" in these and other instances?

This book looks at how we decide. It first considers the nature of the ethical dilemma in business—this conflict between economic and social performance. Ethical dilemmas in management are not simple choices between "right" and "wrong"; they are complex judgments on the balance between economic returns and social damages, complicated by the multiple alternatives, extended consequences, uncertain probabilities, and career implications that are an inherent part of these decisions.

The book then examines three alternative means of arriving at a decision when faced with an ethical conflict:

1. Economic analysis, relying on impersonal market forces.
2. Legal analysis, relying on impersonal social rules.
3. Ethical analysis, relying on personal moral values.

None of these means of analysis is satisfactory by itself. But all together the analyses do form a means of moral reasoning that can help a manager to arrive at a decision that he or she can feel to be "right" and "proper" and "just." The book makes no effort to dictate what is "right" and "proper" and "just"; instead, that is left to the individual's own moral standards of behavior and ethical systems of belief. The intent is to help individuals understand the reasoning process that makes use of these moral standards of behavior and ethical systems of belief so that each individual can form his or her reasoned judgment when faced with a business decision that is, by its very nature, going to injure someone else.

Last, let me say that I am not the only person to have thought about the question of what is "right" and "proper" and "just" in management. There are lots of other theorists and practitioners. I have learned greatly from both groups and should like to acknowledge my debt to Richard DeGeorge (Kansas), Manuel Velasquez (Santa Clara), Thomas Donaldson (Georgetown), Patricia Werhane (Loyola of Chicago), Gerald Cavanagh (Detroit), William Frederick (Pittsburgh), Edwin Epstein (Berkeley), Oliver Williams (Notre Dame), Lisa Newton (Fairfield), Kirk Hanson (Stanford), and Nicholas Steneck (Michigan). I thank you all.

I should also like to very specifically thank Marsha Haas (College of Charleston), Thomas McLaughlin (City University of Seattle), and Sally Power (College of St. Thomas). Their comments on the content and structure of the first edition met that hard-to-achieve reviewer's goal of being both forcefully expressed and helpfully intended. Following their suggestions, I have included 15 new cases, many of which focus on the moral problems encountered by either recent graduates or current students, and I have rewritten Chapter 6 on the important topic of the influence of the senior management upon the moral tone and ethical ambitions of the firm. Let me express my appreciation to the three of you.

LaRue Tone Hosmer

Contents

The Moral Claims of Microeconomic Theory. Pragmatic
Objections to Microeconomic Theory. Theoretic Objections to
Microeconomic Theory.

3 Managerial Ethics and the Rule of Law   72

Law as a Guide to Moral Choice. An Example of Moral Choice.
Law as Combined Moral Judgments. Definition of the Law.
Consistent. Universal. Published. Accepted. Enforced. Relationships
Between the Law and Moral Standards. Formation of the Law:
Individual Processes. Formation of the Law: Group Processes.
Formation of the Law: Social Processes. Formation of the Law:
Political Processes. Conclusions on the Rule of Law as the Basis
for Moral Choice.

4 Managerial Ethics and Normative Philosophy   101

Definition of Normative Philosophy. Ethical Relativism. Eternal
Law. Utilitarianism: A Teleological Theory. Universalism:
A Deontological Theory. Distributive Justice. Personal
Liberty. Conclusions on Normative Philosophy as the Basis for
Moral Choice.

5 Managerial Ethics and Individual Decisions   143

Ethical Analysis and the Lockheed Bribery Case. Ethical Analysis
and a Justifiable Bribery Case. Multiple Analysis and Ethical
Dilemmas. *Pricing of Checking Account Services. Exaggerated or*

Misleading Claims in Advertising. Misuse of Frequent Flyer Discounts and Trips. Working Conditions in a Manufacturing Plant. Customer Service and Declining Product Quality. Work-Force Reductions. Environmental Pollution. Property Tax Reductions. Multiple Analysis and "Drawing the Line".

6 Managerial Ethics and Organizational Design   169

The Wreck of the *Exxon Valdez.* Aftermath of the Wreck. Causes of the Wreck. *Functional and Operating Causes of the Accident. Divisional and Budgetary Causes of the Accident. Corporate and Strategic Causes of the Accident.* Written Code of Ethics to Convey Performance Expectations. Informal Review Process to Advise on Performance Expectations. Reexamination of the Strategy, Structure, Systems and Style. The Moral Responsibilities of Senior Management.

The Ethics of Management

CHAPTER 1

The Nature of Ethics in Management

Ethical issues occur frequently in management. They extend far beyond the commonly discussed problems of bribery, collusion, and theft, reaching into such areas as corporate acquisitions, marketing policies, and capital investments. A large corporation has taken over a smaller one through the common practice of negotiating for the purchase of stock. Then, in merging the two firms, it is found that some of the positions in one are duplicated in the other. Is it right to fire or demote executives holding those duplicate positions, many of whom have served their respective firms for years? A manufacturer that has grown rapidly in an expanding market was helped greatly during that growth by wholesale distributors that introduced its products to retail stores. Now the market has become large enough to make direct distribution from the factory to the store in truckload lots much less expensive, and the market has become competitive enough to make the cost savings from direct distribution very meaningful. Is it proper to change distribution channels? A paper company in northern Maine can generate power and reduce its energy costs by building a large dam on land that it owns, but the dam will block a river that canoeists and fishermen have used for years. Is it fair to ruin recreational opportunities for others?

"Right" and "proper" and "fair" are ethical terms. They express a judgment about behavior toward people that is felt to be just. We believe that there are right and wrong ways to behave toward others, proper and improper actions, fair and unfair decisions. These beliefs are our moral standards. Moral standards differ among individuals because the values upon which they are based differ; and no one can say with certainty that a given moral standard is correct or incorrect provided it can be shown that the standard truly does express an obligation to others, and not just a benefit for ourselves. The problem is that it is difficult, even in the simplest of situations, to distinguish between "us" and "others" and between "benefits" and "obligations," and it is particularly difficult to make this distinction in business management. Why? Various groups are involved in business—managers at different levels and functions, workers of different skills and backgrounds, suppliers of different materials, distributors of different products, creditors of different types, stockholders of different holdings, and citizens of different communities, states, and countries—and a benefit for one may represent the denial of an obligation to another group.

We can illustrate this difficulty with examples from the introductory paragraph. It would seem wrong at first glance to fire executives who happened, through no fault of their own, to hold duplicate positions in the merged firms; yet let us assume that the two companies were in a very competitive industry and that the basic reason for the merger was to become more efficient and to be better able to withstand foreign competitors. What will happen if the staff reductions are not made? Who will be hurt, then, among other managers, workers, suppliers, distributors, creditors, stockholders, and members of the local communities? Who will benefit if the company is unable to survive? Even if survival is not an issue, who will benefit if the company is unable to grow or if it lacks the resources necessary for product research and market development? The basic questions are the same in the other two examples: Who will benefit, and how much? Who will be penalized, and how much? These are not easy questions to answer. In many instances, fortunately, alternatives can be considered. Duplicate managers, instead of being fired, might be retrained and reassigned. Inefficient distributors are a more difficult problem, though a place might be made for them by introducing new products or developing new markets or helping them to participate in the new distribution processes. The dam across the waterway poses the most difficult problem: it either exists or it doesn't, and making it smaller or putting it in a different location does not really resolve the dilemma.

ETHICAL PROBLEMS AS MANAGERIAL DILEMMAS

Ethical problems are truly managerial dilemmas, because they represent a conflict between an organization's economic performance (measured by revenues, costs, and profits) and its social performance (stated in terms of obligations to persons both within and outside the organization). The nature of these obligations is, of course, open to interpretation, but most of us would agree that they include protecting loyal employees, maintaining competitive markets, and producing useful and safe products and services.

Unfortunately, the dilemma of management is that these obligations are costly, both for organizations evaluated by financial standards and for managers subject to financial controls. The manufacturer that distributes directly from the factory to stores will be more profitable and better able to withstand competition than the manufacturer that ships to wholesale warehouses for additional handling and transport. The salesperson, to use a new and more troublesome illustration, who gives small bribes to purchasing agents will have a better record and receive higher commissions than the salesperson who refuses to countenance unethical payments. The design engineer who finds ways to sharply reduce material costs is more likely to be promoted than the design engineer who places product quality and consumer safety above cost considerations. There is a "right" or "proper" or "just" balance between economic performance and social performance, and the dilemma of management comes in finding it. The purpose of this book is to examine the factors that enter into that balance and to consider various theoretical structures—economic theories, legal regulations, and philosophic doctrines—that may assist management in determining it.

It is possible, of course, to ignore the balance between economic and social performance and to argue that the managerial dilemma does not exist. This argument has been advanced from two opposite directions. Some contend that management should concentrate entirely on economic performance. This view is almost a caricature of the 19th-century approach to business, in which coal mines were assumed to be unsafe and steel mills were expected to produce pollution as well as profits. Fortunately, this belief seems to be not at all common today; most managers recognize the impact of their decisions and actions upon the organization and the community. Some people may wish that the managers made other decisions or took other actions, but I think that it is necessary to admit that the recognition exists. There are few executives active now in business firms or nonprofit institutions who do not understand the far-reaching consequences of their decisions and, to some extent, act upon that understanding.

The second view, which is far more widespread, comes from an oversimplification of the issue of social performance. Those who hold this view might say, for example, with some degree of asperity, that "no company should discharge harmful wastes, pay illegal bribes, or produce unsafe products" and might then declare, with an equal degree of satisfaction, that "those ethical difficulties have been resolved—let us go on to the more interesting and nationally critical problems of the proper utilization of our scarce resources." This view ignores the subtlety of ethical issues in management; it assumes that ethical questions have only a "yes" side and a "no" side and that explicit economic benefits and social costs are associated with each of these two alternatives, so that only a very simple level of moral understanding is needed to make the proper choice. In fact, however, ethical questions can have many alternatives, each with different economic and social consequences, some with unknown probabilities of occurrence, and most with personal impacts upon the managers. Let us look at some of these more complex ethical problems.

AN ETHICAL DILEMMA IN
ENVIRONMENTAL PROTECTION

The exhaust from a diesel engine contains approximately 900 chemical compounds. Most of these compounds have been identified, but the environmental effects of only a few of these compounds have been studied. It seems safe to assume that some of the chemical compounds in diesel exhaust are harmful to human health or to air quality. It also seems safe to assume that in total the exhaust from a diesel engine is less harmful than that from a gasoline motor due to the absence of lead compounds—there is some lead even in "lead-free gasoline"—and to the lower levels of nitrous oxides. Every diesel engine manufacturer has a laboratory group that is studying the impact of the exhaust gases upon the general ecological system. Let us assume that in one of these companies this laboratory group finds that a particular compound is very deleterious to roadside vegetation. What are the managers of that company to do?

The managers of this diesel engine manufacturer have a number of choices, all with very uncertain outcomes, that interrelate economic, social, environmental, and personal factors. If they stop producing diesel engines, they will harm their own employees, suppliers, dealers, customers, and owners, and they will probably cause even greater deterioration in air quality as gasoline engines replace the discontinued diesel units. If they develop, at considerable cost, a catalytic converter to reduce or eliminate the harmful compound and then raise their prices, they may be less able to compete within the market. If they absorb the costs of the catalytic converter as a contribution to national welfare, the reduced profits would probably cause increased resistance in labor wage negotiations. In any case, is it ethical to shift the burden from society in general to these workers in particular? "Aha," you retort, "that will not be necessary; the managers can certainly advise the responsible people within the federal government and allow a regulatory agency to establish industry-wide standards, so that all producers will compete with the same cost and price structure." Fine, but now what is to be done about the international market? Forty percent of the diesel engines manufactured in the United States are sold abroad or are installed in domestic equipment that is then sold abroad. If these standards are extended internationally for U.S. producers, they will probably be unable to compete abroad, with all the consequences of that inability upon economies of scale and costs of production for the domestic market. If these standards are not extended internationally for U.S. producers, an implicit statement is made that foreign people are of less worth than people in the United States.

Ethical issues are complex. Let us look at one or two others. Fortunately, these problems are interesting as well as intricate.

AN ETHICAL DILEMMA IN FOREIGN BRIBERY

Bribery is generally considered reprehensible. Even in countries where it is alleged to be common, most people deplore it, except at the lower levels of some governmental bureaucracies where bribes are regarded as part of the compensation system, almost on a level with commissions or gratuities. Probably the principal reason for the widespread condemnation of bribery is its inherent inequity; it is obviously unfair to have special payments and secret influence decide issues that should be decided on their merits. All ethical systems recognize the need for equity; all ethical systems deplore the practice of bribery. It is interesting to note that the earliest written ethical belief, "Crito" in *The Dialogues of Plato*, discussed bribery and recognized the dilemma that an act which is prima facie—that is, at first glance, before considering the full ramifications—considered to be wrong, such as bribery, can result in ends which are prima facie considered to be good, such as the release of prisoners. This same dilemma, though perhaps on a less dramatic scale, exists in management.

Let us look first at a small and almost routine transaction. Assume that the manager of a Brazilian subsidiary of an American company has received a notice that a shipment of repair parts has been received at the Sao Paulo docks and is being held by the customs officials. The common practice is to hire a Brazilian agent who specializes in clearing imports through customs; such agents are considered semiprofessionals, with some legal and financial training, but they are known primarily for their good verbal abilities and their superb negotiating skills. They tend to be quick-witted people who understand the interests of their opponents, and they strive for a fast determination of the applicable import fees and an early release of the impounded goods. After a shipment has been cleared through customs, the agent submits a bill that includes an amount for the duty and a charge for the negotiations. This charge varies, but not with the size of the duty: a commission at a set percentage would be considered "unethical" in Brazil. It is the agent's duty to negotiate the lowest possible fees, and it is considered wrong to force people to choose between their own interests and those of their client. Instead, the charge depends on the time needed to complete the transaction: the quicker the work, the higher the payment. It is assumed that part of the agent's fee has been paid to the customs officials; the larger payments, of course, bring more prompt attention from the officials and much quicker release of the goods. Payments on this basis also serve the interests of the client, for delays in Brazilian customs can extend from two to three months.

In this example, the ethical issue is slightly blurred, partially because there is no proof that bribery payments have been made—though it is logical to assume that some exchange has occurred to gain the attention of the customs officials—and partially because this exchange has been indirect. Managers in the subsidiary of the American company can claim legally that they have not paid bribes, though I am not certain that this claim would be considered defensible by those of us outside the courtroom. The ethical problem, though blurred, seems clear enough: Should a company employ an agent who will probably bribe a government official, resulting in inequitable treatment for others and favored treatment for itself?

Most ethical issues in management are at this apparently simple level: there is a dichotomous, yes or no choice, with relatively clear financial benefits and social obligations associated with each alternative, and the solution proposed is to sensitize people trained in financial analysis to recognize and include social costs in that analysis. But, as stated earlier, this seems to oversimplify the ethical dilemma and to ignore many of the complexities of managerial ethics.

Let us add some of those complexities to the present illustration. Let us assume that the repair parts in question are needed to maintain a communication system, or a manufacturing plant, or even a health-care facility. If the parts are not cleared promptly through customs and a breakdown occurs, people may be inconvenienced because of a failure of the communication system, or they may be unemployed because of a shutdown of the manufacturing plant, or they may suffer death or severe pain because of a breakdown in service at a hospital. Now it becomes clear that the comparison of financial benefits versus social costs is neither as simple nor as obvious as it appeared earlier, for the social ramifications of the decision extend beyond the first level of results into subsequent levels. The consequences of managerial decisions, even on such day-to-day issues as the customs clearance of imported goods, extend throughout society, and these consequences, both positive and negative, have to be included in the original analysis.

Let us also agree that the problem being discussed, paying an indirect bribe for prompt customs clearance, is not truly dichotomous. Numerous alternatives in addition to the obvious yes and no choices are also available. The subsidiary could engage in forward planning and order repair parts far in advance of actual need so that the lengthy delays in customs could be tolerated and the need to pay bribes eliminated. Statistical analysis of the operations, whether of a communication system, a manufacturing plant, or a health-care facility, would indicate a probable demand for repair parts, and numerous mathematical models are available to establish adequate inventory levels, given lengthy delivery times. Another alternative would be to have a corporate attorney negotiate with the customs officials, subject to explicit policy instructions not to pay bribes under any circumstances, and force the officials through legal penalties to clear shipments in the order of their arrival. Yet another alternative would be to obtain repair parts from local suppliers, thus helping to bolster the national economy while avoiding the problems of customs clearance entirely.

Each of these alternatives has a financial cost that we can assume will be somewhat greater than the expenses for the currently minimal bribes, but that cost can be computed. So, on the surface, it would appear that we are now looking at a comparison of financial costs versus social benefits. But, to the manager who has to decide, it is very obvious that here each alternative has a social cost that is more subtle. The inventory models require, for computation, an estimate of the costs of lacking a part that is needed for repairs. The original intent of the management scientists who developed these models was to consider only objective judgments of the costs to the company, but it has become obvious in recent years that the models also have to include subjective estimates of the costs to the employees, the customer, and the general population. Even unsophisticated management science procedures now require some estimate of the costs external to the firm and of the economic damages caused by the firm. In the particular instance being discussed, what cost should be included for Brazilian people who are being inconvenienced when their communication system breaks down due to lack of repair parts? What cost should be included for Brazilian workers who become unemployed and unpaid when their factory is shut down? What cost should be included for Brazilian patients who are untreated when their hospital is unable to function? These are not simple financial estimates; they are extended social costs that are difficult to compute but have to be included in ethical managerial decisions, even when management science procedures are being used. Ethical managerial issues are also posed by the other two alternatives that were suggested—employing a corporate attorney to force the customs official to adhere to the provisions of the law even if this resulted in court actions and civil penalties against those officials, and purchasing repair parts within the country, even if this required an uneconomic transfer of both capital and technology to a local company. If the former alternative were chosen, a corporate attorney would be hired to impose American standards of bureaucratic integrity upon the Brazilian civil service. At one level, there is the question whether an American firm has the right to force its view upon others. At a more subtle level, we have to look at the social structure of Brazil. Corporate attorneys there tend to come from the wealthier families, while customs officials are members of a much poorer class. In essence, the company would be transferring payments from the poor to the rich and thereby helping to maintain the inequitable social divisions of South America.

The sourcing of repair parts within the country seems an attractive alternative superficially, but it involves moving jobs from the United States to Brazil, along with the proprietary technology and some capital investment. That movement will doubtless be directly counter to employee expectations—if not union contracts—in the United States. Until recently, union negotiators seldom foresaw the possibility of foreign purchases of complex components, believing the necessary technical skills to be absent in low-wage-rate areas. With the continual development of advanced technologies in less developed countries that situation has changed. Using foreign labor may create worker hardships in the United States.

Having examined the extended impacts, multiple alternatives, and mixed outcomes that seem to be inherently associated with ethical decisions in management, we will now consider two additional levels of complexity, and then it will be possible to present a series of conclusions on the nature of ethics in management. The fourth level of complexity is the uncertain consequences of managerial decisions. When a managerial decision is made, it is seldom clear exactly what the outcome of that decision will be, and unfortunately the greatest clarity often seems to be linked to the least ethical action, judged by prima facie standards. In the simple illustration that has been used throughout this section—the payment of an indirect bribe to facilitate the clearance of repair parts through customs—it is reasonable to assume that if the bribe is paid, the shipment will be released. The Brazilian customs officials may be unfamiliar with the cynical 19th-century American aphorism, "An honest man is one who, once purchased, stays bought." However, they doubtless understand that unless agreements concluded with the import agents are observed (one hesitates to say "honored" in this context), further negotiations and payments will be impaired. An equal certainty does not extend to the other alternatives.

Uncertainty is even present in the alternative of an expanded repair parts inventory. We have all been annoyed by delays in repair service caused by inadequate inventories; such inadequacies can stem from management inattention, financial constraints, or pure chance. Most of them can probably be ascribed to the first two causes, but a combination of rare events is always a possibility, particularly in repair service where numerous parts are needed for each operating system, where a given region or area contains multiple operating systems, and where obtaining repair parts is subject to extensive delays. Murphy's Law has not been repealed by management science, it has just been partially circumvented; and even large, economically unjustifiable inventories cannot prevent downtime caused by a lack of parts. This is the dilemma that the manager of every repair service intuitively understands: he or she is unable to assure complete protection against failure. That inability is annoying when the parts are needed by a communication system, troublesome when they are needed by a manufacturing plant, and depressing when they are needed by a hospital.

Formal procedures for including uncertainty are available for inventory-planning models, based upon the statistical analysis of historical operating patterns, but such procedures are not applicable to the other two alternatives that were suggested, since relevant data are lacking. It is not at all clear what would happen if an attorney threatened or instituted legal action against customs officials in Brazil. Those officials might release the shipments promptly to avoid harassment in a legal system they did not understand—or papers might be lost, hearings delayed, and shipments misdirected as the same officials created havoc in an import system they understood very well.

An incident illustrates how the legal system can be confounded. I have been told that a Brazilian attorney watched customs officials unwrap, inspect, and clear for import 20 fuel injectors for large diesel engines. The fuel injector is a precisely machined component in the engine; it tends to wear out because of the high pressures that are required in operation. The fuel injectors were inspected, cleared, shipped, and stored. After the first one was installed on an engine, it was found that a pinch of very fine sand had been deposited in the input ports of each unit. All of them had to be scrapped. Sabotage is not common, in Brazil or elsewhere, but it does happen; a manager has to recognize that it can occur and plan for that possibility.

It is also not at all clear what would happen if a local company were selected and trained to produce the needed repair parts inside the country. The training would probably extend far beyond simple instruction in manual skills, requiring the importation of advanced equipment for both production and testing and the explanation of managerial processes in operations scheduling, test evaluation, and quality control. Despite technological and financial assistance from the parent firm, and assuming goodwill and effort on the part of all others, the exportation of highly technical processes is often unsuccessful; it requires a degree of precision and skill that may be outside the culture of the receiving firm.

In summary, it is not certain that the necessary repair parts can be manufactured in Brazil, despite the investment of money and effort. It is also not certain that they can be imported into Brazil by pressuring the customs officials with legal penalties. It is, however, reasonably certain that these parts can be received promptly by employing an import agent and authorizing the customary payments. Uncertainty seems to be a constant companion of the ethical approach to management.

The last level of complexity that we will consider is the personal involvement of the managers. It seems reasonable to assume that this involvement is partially an emotional concern with the ethical dilemma—no one likes to pay bribes or to conspire in their indirect payment—but that it is primarily a practical worry over the impact of ethical issues upon the manager's salary, promotion, and career. Managers, particularly those in autonomous operating units some distance from the corporate headquarters, are expected to "get things done" and to "keep things running." They are not told that they are free to do whatever is necessary to accomplish those goals, and many corporations have codes of ethics and specific functional policies that attempt to preclude many actions, but the managerial controls tend to emphasize financial results and not ethical decisions. The ability of managers to "keep things running" will show up on the control system during the next quarter, while the decisions and actions that enabled them to do so have to be explained only verbally, if at all. Managerial controls tend to focus on the short term and the obvious, but they are often used in judgments about longer-term salaries and promotions.

Managers in almost all companies operate within the constraints of a control system. Certainly, managers in all well-run companies operate within such constraints, and it does no harm to assume that the American manufacturing firm with a troubled subsidiary in Brazil is well run. The controls are normally based upon a comparison of actual results with planned objectives. These objectives are usually set by an extrapolation of past results, with some adjustment for current conditions and local problems derived through discussions between the responsible managers. Both results and objectives are focused primarily on financial measures such as sales revenues, variable costs, fixed expenses, and the resultant profits or losses, because those are the figures that are available from the accounting records. Assuming that the Brazilian subsidiary has this kind of control system, that failure to provide adequate repair service will eventually affect sales revenues, and assuming that payments to the import agent can be classified as a legitimate and necessary business expense, it must be a rare manager who would not say, "Damn the company for putting me into this position," and make the call authorizing indirect payments. This is unfortunate, but it happens, and I think that it is necessary to understand the behavioral implications of the control system that helps to make it happen.

CHARACTERISTICS OF ETHICAL PROBLEMS IN MANAGEMENT

What does all this mean? We have examined in great detail a relatively minor problem faced by a worried manager primarily to consider in detail the actual nature of the ethical dilemma in management. From that examination, five conclusions concerning the complexity of managerial ethics can be stated simply and directly:

1. Most ethical decisions have extended consequences. The results of managerial decisions and actions do not stop with the first-level consequences. Rather, these results extend throughout society, and that extension constitutes the essence of the ethical argument: the decisions of managers have an impact upon others—both within the organization and within the society—that is beyond their control and that therefore should be considered when the decisions are made. Bribes change governmental processes. Pollution affects environmental health. Unsafe products destroy individual lives. There is little disagreement here; most people recognize the extended consequences of managerial actions. The disagreement results from the existence of the multiple alternatives, mixed outcomes, uncertain occurrences, and personal implications that complicate the decision process leading to those actions.

2. Most ethical decisions have multiple alternatives. It is commonly thought that ethical issues in management are primarily dichotomous, a yes and no choice but no other alternatives. Should a manager pay a bribe or not? Should a factory pollute the air or not? Should a company manufacture unsafe products or not? Although a dichotomous framework presents the ethical issues in sharp contrast, it does not accurately reflect the managerial dilemma. As has been seen in the simple illustration of bribery payments for import clearances, and as will be shown in numerous other examples throughout this text, multiple alternatives have to be considered in making ethical choices.

3. Most ethical decisions have mixed outcomes. It is commonly thought that ethical issues in management are largely antithetical, with directly opposed financial returns and social costs. Pay an indirect bribe, but maintain the sales volume of imported goods through prompt delivery. Cause some air or water pollution, but avoid the costs of installing and operating pollution control equipment. Design a slightly unsafe product, but reduce the material and labor costs of manufacture. Like the dichotomous framework, the antithetical model for outcome evaluation presents the ethical issues in sharp focus but does not accurately portray the managerial dilemma. Social benefits and costs as well as financial revenues and expenses are associated with almost all of the alternatives in ethical choices.

4. Most ethical decisions have uncertain consequences. It is commonly thought that ethical issues in management are free of risk or doubt, with a known outcome for each alternative. Pay the bribe, and receive the imported goods promptly. Invest in pollution control equipment, and the emissions will be reduced X percent at Y costs of operation. Produce an absolutely safe product at an additional cost of Z dollars per unit. A deterministic model—that is, one without probabilities—simplifies the process of analysis, but it does not accurately describe the managerial dilemma. It was not at all clear what consequences would follow from the alternatives considered to avoid paying indirect bribes to Brazilian customs officials; it is not at all clear what consequences will follow from most ethical choices.

5. Most ethical decisions have personal implications. It is commonly thought that ethical issues in management are largely impersonal, divorced from the lives and careers of the managers. Many people believe that prima facie ethical decisions in a given operation may reduce the profits of the company but not the executives' salaries or their opportunities for promotion. Managerial controls, however, are designed to record financial results of the operations, not the ethical quality of the decisions that led to those results, and most incentive systems are based upon these controls. Maintain the dollar sales of imported goods at expected levels, and despite slightly increased expenses for indirect bribes, the quarterly review will be pleasant and remunerative. Delay the installation of pollution control equipment, and the return on invested capital will be close to the planned percentage. Redesign the product to reduce material and labor costs, and profit margins and the chances of promotion will increase. An impersonal model certainly simplifies the process of decision on ethical issues, but it far from accurately describes the managerial dilemma. Individual benefits and costs, as well as financial and social benefits and costs, are associated with most of the alternatives in ethical decisions.

EXAMPLES OF ETHICAL PROBLEMS IN MANAGEMENT

Ethical problems in management are complex because of the extended consequences, multiple alternatives, mixed outcomes, uncertain occurrences, and personal implications. Ethical problems in management are also pervasive, because managers make decisions and take actions that will affect other people. If those decisions and actions affect other people adversely, if they hurt or harm those people in ways beyond their individual control, then we have an ethical problem that requires some degree of moral analysis in addition to the more common economic analysis. What are some of these ethical problems? Let us look at a few, bearing in mind that the moral content of each differs, and that each of us will differ in our view of the moral severity of that content. That is, using the issues discussed in the introductory paragraph of this chapter, some of us may feel that it is morally wrong to discharge long-service employees following a merger, to replace wholesale distributors as the market matures, or to build a power-generating dam that will block recreational access to a river. Others of us may feel that some decisions of this kind are morally wrong but that others—particularly the dam on company-owned property— are morally right. Still other people may argue that while these decisions have unfortunate consequences, they are nonetheless all morally right.

Moral standards differ between individuals because the ethical systems of belief—the values or priorities, the convictions that people think are truly important and upon which their moral standards are based—also differ. These beliefs depend upon each person's family background, cultural heritage, church association, educational experience, and other factors. The differences in ethical beliefs are not important at this stage of the discussion; they will be examined in the next three chapters. What is important at this stage is to recognize that each of the decisions and actions that will be described briefly below can affect other people adversely, can hurt or harm them in ways beyond their control, and consequently, have a moral content. The condition of hurt or harm to others in ways beyond their control is the essential element in the ethical dilemma of management. That condition is present in all the examples that follow.

Before going on to describe these additional ethical problems in management, let me state two qualifications and provide a personal explanation. First, the intent is not to describe every possible instance in which managerial decisions and actions can hurt or harm individuals in ways beyond their control. Rather, the intent is to provide a limited number of examples that show the pervasive nature of ethical problems in management and furnish general topics for subsequent discussion of the various analytical means for reaching decisions when confronted with such problems.

Second, the intent is not to describe dramatic and well-publicized instances of management decisions that were clearly unethical and often illegal as well. The president of Lockheed did pay $3.2 million to various government officials and representatives of the prime minister of Japan to ensure the purchase of 20 passenger planes by the Japanese national airline.[1] Senior members of management at General Dynamics did add $63 million of improper overhead expenses, including country club memberships and dog kennel fees, to defense contracts during the period 1979–82.[2] Regional managers at E. F. Hutton did issue bank overdrafts that gave Hutton the interest-free use of up to $250 million and cost banks as much as $8 million.[3] Marketing executives at a company manufacturing artificial eye lenses for cataract-replacement surgery did, according to a report issued by a subcommittee of Congress, provide "free use of a yacht off Florida, travel in Europe, all-expense paid and week-long training seminars in the Bahamas, second homes, and cash rebates" for buying their lenses rather than the lenses of their competitors.[4] These unethical actions did occur, but few people would defend them except perhaps to say that one has to adopt foreign business practices when doing business abroad, or that the Defense Department is too large to be properly managed, or that the banks should have recognized what was happening much earlier, or that health-care costs are clearly out of control. The intent here is to look not at such actions, but at a range of issues at the operating, middle, and strategic levels of management and in most of the functional and technical specialties. Some of these issues require decisions by senior executives, but most are the routine, even mundane decisions and actions that lower-level managers—and recent graduates of business schools—face on an almost daily basis.

Last, and this is the personal explanation, I am going to use anonymous quotations to amplify and support some of the descriptions of ethical problems in management. This is in direct contradiction to the research rule that sources should always be cited, so that the validity of the findings can be substantiated. However, I believe that in this instance the use of anonymous quotations may be justified. It is difficult to get examples of ethical problems at the lower and middle levels of management. Managers at those levels do not like to discuss the ethical dilemmas they have faced, for the obvious reason that those discussions can adversely affect their careers. They will discuss them only with persons who are known to have an interest in the area, who perhaps can help them in the resolution of the problem, and who certainly will maintain confidentiality. I have taught at three schools of business administration over the past 12 years, and at each of these institutions I have either conducted short seminars or used short cases in elective classes that revealed my interest in the ethics of management. Former students from those seminars and classes occasionally contact me when troubled about particular practices that seem to be accepted as ordinary business routines within their companies. They write or speak with the assumption of confidentiality, and so I cannot identify them. Yet their descriptions are much more vivid, and probably valid, than my own because they have been part of the problems they are describing, and so I wish to include the descriptions. That is the reason I believe the use of anonymous quotations is justified in these examples. Now, on to the problems.

Pricing Level

Price, it would seem, should be a purely economic decision based upon cost and demand. Yet the pricing level selected can have harmful effects upon some customers. In banking, for example, under the combined impact of deregulation by the government and competition from other financial service firms, it has become common to pay fairly high rates of interest on customer deposits. But the benefits of those rates go primarily to the customers with the larger bank balances. To offset the increased interest that must be paid to attract the larger deposits and to reflect the actual costs of service, most banks have raised the fees they charge smaller customers.

I have been asked to do a study of the pricing for our checking account services. Other banks in the area now charge $0.10 for each transaction for accounts that don't maintain a $1,000 balance and an additional $5 per month for the very small accounts with a balance that falls under $300. That makes a lot of sense, economically. We just barely break even now servicing the medium-sized accounts, and we lose money on the smaller ones. The proposed price changes would mean that our returns would be equal for all three sizes of accounts.

But there is a problem. We are an urban bank. Many of our customers are retired, on Social Security. Five dollars a month is a major expense for them; it represents a couple of meals that they are not going to eat. Most of them don't have the money to maintain a $300 balance. They're older, and frightened of carrying cash. I don't think that it is right to, in essence, deny checking account services to older people, but I don't know what to do about it. You see, if we don't have the same rate structure as the other banks, we will get all of these older and unprofitable customers.

When I left [name of the business school], I was determined that I would maintain my personal standards in everything that I did. Yet in the first year I am going to recommend a policy that I think is morally wrong. (Statement of former student)

Advertising Messages

Truth in advertising is a complex issue, and an emotional one. A rigidly truthful television or magazine ad, every statement of which is supported by a reference to a scientific study, would be incredibly dull and probably ineffective. A totally untruthful television or magazine ad, with wildly exaggerated claims, would be illegal and probably equally ineffective. Varying degrees of truthfulness and deception lie between those two extremes. The problem for one former student was where to draw the line along that spectrum.

Despite our reputation as hucksters, 90 percent of what we do in advertising is legitimate, and based upon valid market analysis. For the large majority of our clients, we act more as marketing consultants than as advertisers. Our ads may be dull; they are generally unimaginative; and they often present a very one-sided view of things, but they are seldom designed to be deliberately untruthful.

It's the other 10 percent that I worry about. We have a client who says that they want a campaign with more "bite"; bite to them means more pull, more attraction to the buyer, even if that attraction is blatantly untrue and totally misrepresented. They are in the financial services industry, but they want to sell their products as if they were headache remedies or arthritis rubs. "Up 387 percent over the past three years" is the heading they have on a mutual fund ad, and that is an accurate statement only if you stay strictly within that time frame; over the past five years the fund has not kept pace with the growth in the Dow Jones Averages. "8½ percent interest" is the heading they have on a money market fund; there is a small asterisk, and down at the bottom of the page a footnote that explains the 8½ percent is for the first month only. "Insured by [name of an insurance company]" is a phrase they want on every ad that mentions customer accounts; that insurance company is their wholly owned and poorly funded subsidiary. We do the work for them, but I don't like it. (Statement of former student)

Product Promotions

Advertising is one form of promotion; another is the use of "free" gifts and price rebates to attract customers. Under the impact of deregulation, airlines have developed product promotions in the form of additional flights and vacation lodgings for "frequent flyers"—passengers who exceed a given mileage on a particular airline each year. Most of the frequent flyers travel on business, yet the benefits are given to the traveler who decides what airline will be used, not to the company that generates the volume of traffic and pays for the tickets, and the cost of those benefits is borne by the nonbusiness traveler, who generally flies much less often and is usually much less able to bear the additional expense.

There are executives in our company who will select a flight based upon the frequent flyer benefits, not upon the cost to the company or the time spent in the air. The man for whom I work is probably the greatest offender; he gets me and others, when we fly, to use his card so that he accumulates the mileage, and the freebies.

Our company has a corporate code of conduct, and the chairman gets us all together once a year and talks about the high standards of [name of the company], yet here is an executive ripping everybody off, and nobody cares. Probably the chairman approves; he always uses one of the corporate jets for his own vacation travel. (Statement of former student)

Working Conditions

The working conditions for many manual and clerical employees are less than ideal. Temperature, humidity, or noise levels may be too high; ventilation and lighting may be too low, and fumes and dust are still found in some workplaces. The most harmful of these conditions, along with the obvious safety hazards, have been outlawed by state and federal laws, but there are still many opportunities to improve working conditions for hourly employees. Here is a former student who felt that it would harm his career to make such improvements.

I think that all MBAs, and I'll include the BBAs too, should be forced as part of their education to work in a steel stamping plant or a grey iron foundry. The noise, the heat, the fumes, and the pace of work are close to intolerable. If there aren't enough places for all of them in a stamping plant or an iron foundry, you could put the balance of them "out on the line" [on the assembly line in an automobile factory].

We have executives in this company who just don't understand what it is like to work under these conditions. Their offices are in New York, and they only come out here a couple of times a year to tell us that we're falling behind on the profit plan. I could put in a capital request to improve some of the worst conditions, but I would have to fight to get it approved. I'm not certain I want to make that effort; people who fight for capital projects that don't show a substantial internal rate of return tend not to get promoted around here. (Statement of former student)

Customer Service

Declining product quality has been a problem in many industries for a number of years. Declining product quality in the automobile industry results in "lemons," new cars with major defects that can create substantial hardships for the buyers, who cannot depend upon these cars for transportation to and from work or to and from medical appointments, shopping trips, family gatherings, and so on.

> I work in the marketing department at [name of an auto company], calling on dealers. Customers with mechanical problems on new cars are supposed to go first to the dealer, then to the company, and finally, if both of those fail, to an arbitration program set up by the Better Business Bureaus in each state. But these procedures don't work. The dealer is paid only a portion of the full cost of warranty repairs, so he tries to get by, doing as little work as possible. I can authorize additional work, but the money comes out of my budget, and you can't run over the budget too often. The result is that the major problems on a customer's car, where we ought to just replace the motor or the transmission or the electrical system, never really do get fixed. We only fix the minor ones. (Statement of former student)

Work Force Reductions

It has become common to reduce the size and the overhead cost of many large companies by discharging some of the employees, to create a "lean and mean" style of management. These "downsizing operations" are generally a response to an increase in competitive pressures, but there is an obvious human cost to the people forced to leave.

> Our company, in August, is going to announce the firing of 24,000 workers, including 15,000 administrative employees. [Name of the company] has always had a reputation for job security, almost lifetime employment, so this announcement is going to come as a shock to many people.
> Of course, the older ones will get the option of early retirement. But the younger ones, in their 30s and 40s, are just going to get a few months' severance pay and some outplacement counseling. I am part of a task force that was set up to decide exactly what benefits should be given to the various longevity classes.
> The senior executives in this company had it easy. When they were at this level, the only problem they had was expansion: finding more people, training them, promoting them. They never had to deal with contraction; they don't recognize the really agonizing nature of the decisions we have to make on an almost daily basis now. (Statement of former student)

Environmental Pollution

Improper disposal of toxic wastes is clearly illegal, yet some companies continue to dump chemicals, despite possible harm to the environment and probable conflict with the law.

> I have been working for [name of the company] for about six months, at their [name of the city] plant. It is common practice here to pour used solvents and cleaning solutions down the storm drain. I asked the plant manager about it, and he said that this is legal in small amounts. I don't think that it is legal, and I don't think that the amounts are that small, but I'm not certain that I want to get involved at this stage of my career. (Statement of former student)

Community Relations

The major employer within a local community has substantial economic power, particularly if the employer has plants in other locations and can move work, and employment, among plants. This economic power often is used in pressing for tax reductions, which can have an obvious impact upon residents of the community by increasing their taxes or decreasing their services.

> [Name of the company] is pushing for a 76 percent tax reduction in [name of the city], where I live. Two years ago it got a 24 percent reduction. Now it is threatening to close the plant unless it gets the full amount. If that reduction goes through, it is going to increase taxes on my house by over $500 a year. I can afford it; I'm well paid. But there are older people around here, and some farmers, who are going to be driven right to the wall. Doesn't the company understand what it is doing? (Statement of former student)

Supplier Relations

Large manufacturing firms have economic power within the communities in which they operate, and against the small suppliers from which they purchase materials, parts, and supplies. Economic power is a difficult concept to define, but it is an easy force to recognize.

> This company has started to play hardball with our suppliers. People in purchasing think nothing of calling up a supplier we've worked with for years, and telling the supplier it has lost the business

unless we get a 7 percent price reduction. Generally we can't make the parts at the prices that purchasing demands, so it is an empty threat. But the supplier doesn't know that; they'll come back with a 3 percent reduction, we'll compromise eventually at 4.2 percent, but we've started to drive somebody else out of business. (Statement of former student)

ANALYSIS OF ETHICAL PROBLEMS IN MANAGEMENT

How do we decide on these and other ethical issues? You may regard some of the examples cited as simple instances of practical management—small suppliers to any large manufacturing company have to be competitive in their price quotations and quality standards, or they will lose the business, and this is particularly true of suppliers to the automobile companies attempting to meet foreign competition. You may regard others as outrageous abuses of power and position—it is hard to justify a 76 percent tax reduction for a corporation that will substantially increase the taxes for community residents, assuming that the original assessments were made equitably. Ethical decisions are easy to make when a person is not directly involved. From a distance, it is easy to review other people's actions and say, "Yes, that is right," or "No, that is wrong."

Ethical decisions are much more difficult to make when a person is directly involved in the situation. Put yourself in the position of the purchasing agent in the automobile company who had to lie to a supplier. Could you do it? If you did not do it, could you continue to work for that company? Put yourself in the position of the person who discovered that the company he worked for was pouring solvents and cleaning fluids down the drain. What would you do?

Suppose you were the former student whose immediate superior required her to cheat the company when purchasing airline tickets, and pass along the benefits to him. Would you do it? This is not truly an ethical dilemma, for there is no conflict between the economic and social performance of the company. This is just a simple case of managerial dishonesty, but your career is probably at risk, and not just if you "blow the whistle" on your boss. At some time in the future, a corporate auditor may find out about this practice and list you as one of the participants.

Suppose you were the former student who had to decide on the proper pricing level for the checking account services offered by your bank. Now, how do you analyze the situation? Is it strictly a matter of costs and margins, or does the bank have some obligation to continue to provide checking account services to older members of the community, and do you have some obligation to make certain that that occurs? Suppose you were asked to set up policy guidelines for the employees to be discharged in a corporate downsizing operation; what standards would you use? Suppose you recognized that your company was producing unsafe products, or making illegal payments; how would you decide what action to take? You need a method of analysis, beyond your intuitive moral standards, when confronted with an immediate ethical problem.

Ethical decisions are not simple choices between right and wrong; they are complex judgments on the balance between the economic performance and the social performance of an organization. In all the instances described above, except for the managerial dishonesty in the example of the airline tickets, the economic performance of the organization, measured by revenues, costs, and profits, will be improved. In all the instances described above, the social performance of the organization—much more difficult to measure, but expressed as obligations to managers, workers, customers, suppliers, distributors, and members of the local community—will be reduced. People are going to be hurt. There has to be a balance between economic and social performance. How do you reach this balance? Three methods of analysis are relevant: economic, legal, and ethical.

Economic Analysis

It is possible to look at many of the problems that have been described as having a definite ethical content from the point of view of microeconomic theory, relying on impersonal market forces to make the decision between economic and social performance. Work force reductions and plant closings are admittedly unpleasant for the workers who lose their jobs, but there is a labor market, and these workers will be employed again, provided they are willing to adjust their wage demands to market conditions. The small wholesalers that are going to be replaced by direct factory shipments to retail stores doubtless feel troubled, but their costs are too high; bring those costs down to a competitive level, and they will not be replaced. The underlying belief is that a society has a limited number of resources and that when consumers are supplied with highest quality goods at lowest possible costs, then those resources are being used as efficiently as possible and members of the society are being served as effectively as possible.

Legal Analysis

It is also possible to look at each of the problems that have an ethical content using the framework of legal theory, relying on impersonal social forces to make the choice between "right" and "wrong." Work force reductions and plant closings are unpleasant, but society has never felt that they were so harmful to the people involved that a law prohibiting them was required. Should they become a major problem, a law can be passed to deal with the situation. The small wholesalers that are going to be replaced doubtless feel bad, but they may have an implicit contract from their earlier service. They can sue in a court of law; if they win, they will not be replaced. The underlying belief here is that a democratic society can establish its own rules and that if people and organizations follow those rules, then members of that society will be treated as justly as possible.

Ethical Analysis

Last, it is possible to look at each of the problems that have a moral content using the structure of normative philosophy, relying on basic principles to make the choice between "right" and "wrong." Work force reductions and plant closings, again, are unpleasant, but we can compute "the greatest good for the greatest number" and decide on that basis. The small wholesalers that are to be replaced are unhappy, but we can set up a rule that every organization, faced with an equivalent situation, has to act in the same way—Kant's Categorical Imperative—and thus achieve consistent and equitable behavior. The belief underlying normative philosophy is that if all the rational men and women in a society acted on the same principles of either beneficency or consistency, then members of that society would be treated as fairly as possible.

Three methods of analysis have been proposed to resolve ethical dilemmas in management. The next three chapters will examine these methods in considerably greater detail.

Notes

1. "Japan: An Aftershock of the Lockheed Affair," *Business Week*, April 12, 1976, p. 43.
2. Roger Bennett, "Profile of Harry Crown, Founder of General Dynamics, Inc.," *New York Times*, June 16, 1985, p. 26f.
3. Scott McMurray, "Battered Broker: E.F. Hutton Appears Headed for Long Siege in Bank-Draft Scheme," *The Wall Street Journal*, July 12, 1985.
4. *Ann Arbor News*, July 19, 1985, p. B1.

CASES

Five Moral Problems Encountered by Members of One BBA Class

Students in a BBA class on the ethics of management at the University of Michigan were asked to submit a written description of a moral problem they had encountered at work over the previous summer. This was a voluntary assignment. Obviously, if they had not encountered a moral problem or if they had encountered one that they felt they could not describe without violating the implied confidence of their former employer, they did not have to participate. Nineteen problems were submitted. The following five were selected by members of the class for discussion at one of the subsequent meetings.

1. *Reporting inaccurate income*: I didn't get the job I wanted, so I worked as a waitress at a restaurant in a vacation resort. We got room and board, the absolute minimum wage (with a charge deducted for the room and board), and tips. Tip income was very good because it was a popular restaurant, right on the shore, with really good food and above-average prices. The owner told us that we had to report our tip income to the IRS, but he also said that he had to provide them with an estimate based upon credit-card charges, and he gave us a figure that was less than half of what I actually made. Now I have to file the return, and I need the money. What figure should I put down?

2. *Misleading retail customers*: I spent the summer working as a telephone sales representative at a travel agency. Customers would call and say where they wanted to go. We would look up flights, times, and fares on the computer and help the customer pick the one that seemed best. That part was all right. But often they asked us to reserve a rental car or find a hotel room. Here the problem was that there generally was a contest for the sales representative who could reserve the most cars from a particular rental firm or send the most clients to a specific hotel chain. All of those companies run contests like that, and the prizes are not cheap. If I booked just 25 clients for [name of a car rental firm] during one month, my name would be put in a drawing for $2,500. If I booked 100 clients, the drawing was for $10,000. If I booked 200, I received a three-day Florida vacation free; there was no drawing. All of the other clerks participated in the contests, and the owner didn't seem to mind. The problem, of course, was that the rates to the customers were higher than they would have been had we searched for the best deal for them rather than the best prize for us. The other clerks said I was crazy not to participate. Should I have participated?

3. *Misleading industrial customers*: I worked in the office of a company that distributed repair parts for heavy machinery throughout northern Michigan. When somebody would call in for a part, we would look up the number, price, and inventory level on the computer. The boss told us always to say that we had the part in stock, even if the inventory level showed that we were out, that we didn't have any left. His argument was that we could always get the part from Chicago in a day or two and that a day or two was not going to hurt anyone. I didn't like it because it meant that I had to lie to somebody about once a day. What do you think I should have done?

4. *Reporting employee theft*: I worked in the shipping bay of a company that manufactured house paint. House paint in 1-gallon cans is a product you can sell easily in your neighborhood if you can get it out the factory door; everyone needs paint. House paint in 1-gallon cans is also an easy product to get out the factory door; it's a big volume product, and no one seems to keep exact track of the numbers. When you are making up the pallets to load a truck (the cans of paint were put in cartons that held four cans, and then 20 cartons were strapped onto a wooden pallet that could be handled by a forklift), you just set aside a couple of cans. Then, when the foreman is on break and the office people are all working in the front of the building, you just carry it out and put it in the trunk of your car. Most of the shipping crew did that once or twice a week. They felt the company owed it to them. I didn't do it because I didn't want to run the risk of being caught and having that put on my record. But I didn't object when they gave me a couple of cans to use on my mother's home. And I didn't tell the management of the company about it, either. What should I have done?

5. *Misusing employee time*: This did not happen last summer; it happened a couple of summers ago. I was part of the maintenance crew for the Parks and Recreation Department in the town where I lived. We mowed the grass on the parks and athletic fields, and picked up the trash and did some painting and repair work. The problem was that we not only did the parks and athletic fields, but we also did the lawns and gardens of some of the people in the city government, the school system, and the athletic department. I mowed the lawn of the football coach every week until practice started. He used to tell me I'd never make the team unless I could move faster on the football field than I did on his front lawn, but he always gave me a glass of lemonade and a $5 tip when I was finished. I never thought about it until I took this course, but maybe it wasn't right to use city employees to work on private property.

Five Moral Problems Encountered by Members of One MBA Class

Students in an MBA class on the ethics of management at the University of Michigan were asked to submit a written description of a moral problem they had encountered at work over the previous summer. This was a voluntary assignment. Obviously, if they had not encountered a moral problem or if they had encountered one that they felt they could not describe without violating the implied confidence of their prior employers, they did not have to participate. Twenty-three problems were submitted. The following five were selected by members of the class for discussion at one of the subsequent meetings.

1. *Telling lies at a market research firm*: I was working for a market research firm in Chicago over the summer. We had an assignment to gather information from companies that used a line of industrial products. This was confidential data (on usage rate, price sensitivity, etc.), and people won't fill out written questionnaires on that type of information. We had to use a telephone survey, for people will generally say much more than they intend to over the telephone if you can get them talking about the topic. We still weren't getting the information the project director wanted, so he told all of us who were doing the survey to say that we were college students gathering the information for a term paper.

2. *Providing gifts at a wholesale distributor*: I was working for a company that supplied packaging materials throughout Ohio. It was just a sales job, but there was a good commission structure, so I could make a lot of money if I was successful. Packaging materials are close to a commodity. You can buy the same boxes and fillers and tape from just about anyone, at just about the same price. The suppliers tend to compete on service to the customer and on gifts to the purchasing agent. Not all of the purchasing agents are the same, but many of them will tell you exactly what they want: a new TV for their rec room, a pair of tickets to a ball game, a set of tires for their car. You either give them what they want, or you don't get the order.

3. *Falsifying reports at a consulting firm*: Much of managerial consulting is not done for the purpose of helping one company compete against other companies within the same industry. Much of it is done for the purpose of helping one group within a company compete against other groups within the same company. You have one group within a company who wants to use a particular technology, or to develop a specific product, and you are hired to provide support for their project. It is clearly understood at the start what the conclusions of the report will be. If you develop some information during the study that contradicts that conclusion, you explain it to the group that arranged to have you hired, but you don't put that information in the final report to the company without the permission of the people from your group.

4. *Firing employees at a chain store*: I was working for a discount chain store that was expanding very rapidly. I was the assistant manager for a new store that was opening in the suburbs of Richmond, Virginia. There is an awful lot of work to be done in opening a new store; you have to order the merchandise, and when it comes in you have to check it off against the right orders, put it in the right racks and on the right shelves, add the right price tags, and generally keep things organized despite the chaos of last-minute construction and cleaning. I was helped by five really good people, who had been convinced to move from other stores in the chain because this was billed as a "training program" for management. We worked long hours. We got the job done. One week after the store opened, I was told to find a reason to fire three of them because "we only have room for two trainees." When I objected I was told, "Hey, there's no problem. They can go back to the jobs they came from."

5. *Taking company property at an accounting firm*: I spent the summer working at the office of a Big Six accounting firm in Denver. The attitude of the people in that office was "anything goes." Expense accounts were a joke. Nobody expected you to submit a receipt, and the result was that half of the employees cheated. People used company telephones for personal long-distance calls, not just occasionally but all the time. Pencils, pens, magic markers, and writing paper disappeared continually. When we left at the end of the summer to come back to school, two of the other summer interns took enough office supplies to last for the rest of the year. I never took anything, but I never told any of the senior partners either. I didn't know what I should do.

Class Assignment. Decide whether or not the situations described in these five very short cases are wrong. If you decide that they are indeed wrong, be prepared to say why you think so.

1. Then, start thinking about how these situations developed. Do the senior executives at each firm know what is happening?

2. What, if anything, could you do about these situations (if you were the person involved) beyond saying "I quit"?

The Good Life at RJR Nabisco

RJR Nabisco was formed June 1, 1985, as a result of a merger between R. J. Reynolds Tobacco Company and National Brands Corporation. National Brands was itself the result of an earlier merger between National Biscuit Company (crackers and cereals) and Standard Brands (packaged foods).

The products of RJR Nabisco are generally well-known. They include Camel, Doral, Salem, Vantage, and Winston cigarettes; Ritz, Premium, and Triscuit crackers; Oreo, Chips Ahoy, and Newton cookies; Fleischmanns and Blue Bonnet margarines; Shredded Wheat and Cream of Wheat cereals; Planters peanuts, Life Saver mints, Baby Ruth candy bars, Royal gelatins, Del Monte canned fruits, Grey Poupon mustard, and Milk Bone dog food.

Since the merger, the sales of RJR Nabisco have steadily increased, helped by the strong cash flow from the tobacco products. It is said that cigarettes and pipe tobacco are ideal "cash cows"; that is, they have high margins and steady sales in a mature market, and consequently they provide excess cash, which can be used for other corporate purposes. The excess cash provided by the cigarettes was used at RJR Nabisco to promote the food products, which in turn achieved high margins and expanding sales in a growth market.

The profits of RJR Nabisco expanded even more rapidly than did sales. The following simplified income statement shows this growth in millions of dollars:

	1985	1986	1987	1988
Sales revenues	11,622	15,102	15,766	16,956
Cost of goods sold	6,024	7,920	8,221	8,786
S & A expenses	3,646	4,842	4,991	5,322
Financial costs	380	660	848	577
Income taxes	662	718	527	893
After-tax profits	910	962	1,179	1,393

The steady tobacco cash flow and the expanding corporate profits funded a life-style at the corporate headquarters of RJR

Nabisco that was described in *The Wall Street Journal* as "a monument of free-spending, nouveau-riche excess."[1]

Executives were very well paid. Mr. F. Ross Johnson, the chairman and chief executive officer, received $3.5 million in 1988. The next 31 executives (whose salaries were published in total, not individually, in the 10K annual report for that year) each received an average salary of $458,000.

Executives also received numerous perks. All of the senior managers at corporate headquarters, and many of the functional and technical people at the divisional offices, were given an allowance of $10,000 a year for estate planning, tax assistance, and investment counseling. Everyone at the managerial rank received at least one country club membership and at least one company car. Executives could select their own country club and their own car model. Some managers received multiple club memberships; Mr. Johnson held the record with more than 24 club memberships spread across the country. Some managers selected very luxurious cars; the record was a special Mercedes-Benz said to have cost over $200,000.

Office decorations at the corporate headquarters matched the managerial salaries, perks, and cars. *The Wall Street Journal* reported that Mr. Johnson's office included a $51,000 vase, a $36,000 table, and a $100,000 rug.[2] Expensive furnishings even extended to the corporate jet hangar at the Atlanta airport.

The RJR Nabisco jet hangar was not a sheet metal building of the type that is commonly seen at airports. Instead, it was a three-story building of tinted glass, surrounded by $250,000 in landscaping. A visitor entered through a tall open atrium, with a roof made of glass panels, floors laid in Italian marble, and walls paneled with Dominican mahogany. $600,000 in furniture was spread through the pilots' lounge and control room, which were also decorated with $100,000 in paintings and statuary.

RJR Nabisco employed 36 pilots and co-pilots, and maintained 10 corporate jets in a fleet commonly known as either the RJR Air Force or Air Johnson. The pilots and planes were used to carry managers to workday meetings and inspection tours, of course, but they were also used to bring sports figures, entertainers, and elected officials to Atlanta for weekend outings. The sports figures and entertainers were paid to be representatives for the company, but spent much of their time playing golf and socializing with the senior executives.

(Mr. Johnson) took excellent care of them, paying more for occasional public appearances than for an average senior vice president: (Don) Meredith got $500,000 a year, (Frank) Gifford $413,000 plus a New York office and apartment, golfer Ben Crenshaw $400,000, and golfer Fuzzy Zoeller $300,000. The king was Jack Nicklaus, who commanded $1 million a year.[3]

It was said that many of the representatives for RJR Nabisco did very little "representing". Jack Nicklaus, for example, refused to make more than six appearances a year, he didn't like to play golf with RJR Nabisco's largest customers, or meet with them at the evening cocktail parties and dinners.

Then there was the O. J. Simpson problem. Simpson, the football star and sports announcer, was being paid $250,000 a year but was a perennial no-show at RJR events. So was Don Mattingly of the New York Yankees, who also pulled down a quarter million. Johnson didn't care. Subordinates took care of those and other problems. He was having a grand time. "A few million dollars," he always said, "are lost in the sands of time."[4]

Class Assignment.   In your opinion, is this life-style of the senior executive officers at a major U.S. corporation "right" or "just" or "fair"? Be prepared to support your belief; don't just say yes or no. Why is it right or why is it wrong? Then answer the following questions:

1. What was the responsibility of the board of directors of RJR Nabisco relative to the expenditures of corporate funds for the management salaries and perquisites, for the airport building, and for the professional athletes?
2. What was the responsibility of Ernst and Whinney, public accountant for RJR Nabisco, relative to the expenditures of corporate funds for management salaries and perquisites, for the airport building, and for the professional athletes?

Notes

1. *The Wall Street Journal,* January 4, 1990, p. B1.
2. Ibid.
3. B. Burrough and J. Helyar, *Barbarians at the Gate: The Fall of RJR Nabisco* (New York: Harper & Row, 1990), p. 94.
4. Ibid.

Managerial Ethics and Microeconomic Theory

We are concerned in this book with ethical dilemmas: decisions and actions faced by managers in which the economic performance and the social performance of the organization are in conflict. These are instances in which someone to whom the organization has some form of obligation—employees, customers, suppliers, distributors, stockholders, or the general population in the area where the company operates—is going to be hurt or harmed in some manner, while the company is going to profit. The question is how to decide: how to find a balance between economic performance and social performance when faced by an ethical dilemma.

A balance is necessary. It is not possible, given the increasingly competitive nature of the business world, always to decide in favor of social performance. It is not possible always to keep in place surplus employees following a merger. It is not possible always to retain obsolete distributors when the economics of the industry have changed. It is not possible always to delay building a dam for power generation because it will destroy recreational opportunities for local residents.

On the other side, however, it is not possible always to decide in favor of economic performance. We can all picture a manager murmuring something about a need to be tough in the three instances above and then firing the surplus employees, replacing the obsolete distributors, and building the new dam. But that was the reason for listing the other ethical dilemmas faced by recent graduate of business schools. Is it possible always to disregard older people, living on fixed incomes, when making a product or pricing decision? Is it possible always to disregard potential customers, and an obligation to be truthful to them, when designing an advertising program? Is it possible always to disregard unpleasant if not hazardous working conditions for production employees in planning capital improvements at a manufacturing plant? If these illustrations at the operating level are not enough, we can move on to the more dramatic examples at the corporate or strategic level that were listed briefly in the previous chapter. Is it right to bribe foreign political leaders to ensure the purchase of the company's products? Is it right to overbill the Defense Department for large, nonessential expenditures to increase the company's profits? Is it right to make fictitious deposits at banks to earn $8 million of interest? Is it right to offer free vacation trips and cash payments to surgeons to sell nearly $200 million of cataract-replacement lenses?

I think that we can all agree, in some of the instances above, that "No, it is not right." At some point along that vector of examples, listed generally in a ranking of increasing moral severity, people's opinions change from "Yes, that seems to be all right" to "No, that is definitely wrong." It is a question of where to draw the line. It is a question of how to balance the economic versus the social performance of the firm.

There are three forms of analysis that can help in drawing the line, that can assist in reaching a decision on the proper balance between economic and social performance. These forms of analysis are economic, based upon impersonal market forces; legal, based upon impersonal social forces; and philosophical, based upon personal principles and values. In this chapter we are going to look at economic analysis, based upon impersonal market forces.

THE MORAL CONTENT OF MICROECONOMIC THEORY

Economic analysis as a means of finding the proper or moral balance between the economic and social performance of a business firm may seem to you to be an anomaly, an impossibility. That is not true; there is a definite moral content to microeconomic theory.

For many persons, the concept of morality in microeconomics—the theory of the firm—is a contradiction in terms; they learned the theory as a logical and mathematical approach to markets and prices and production, devoid of moral substance. As a result of this education, most noneconomists, and perhaps a few economists as well, appear to focus almost entirely on profit maximization. They view the theory as descriptive, designed to rationalize the behavior of business managers, and believe that such single-minded pursuit of profit automatically excludes any consideration of environmental health, worker safety, consumer interests, or other "side issues." Overconcentration on profits doubtless has resulted in these and other problems within our society, but that is neither a consequence nor a corollary of microeconomic theory. Microeconomic theory, in its more complete form, addresses these issues and includes ethical as well as economic precepts.

Microeconomic theory in its complete form is more a normative theory of society than a descriptive theory of the firm. Profit maximization is a part of the theory, but it is only a part, and certainly not the central focus—though it must be admitted, and this adds to the lack of understanding, that techniques for profit maximization occupy a central portion of the curriculum at many schools of business administration. The central focus of the larger theory of society is the efficient utilization of resources to satisfy consumer wants and needs. At economic equilibrium—and an essential element in reaching equilibrium throughout the entire economic system is the effort by business managers to balance marginal increases in revenues against marginal increases in costs, which automatically results in optimal profits for the firm within market and resource constraints—it is theoretically possible to achieve Pareto Optimality.

Pareto Optimality refers to a condition in which the scarce resources of society are being used so efficiently by the producing firms, and the goods and services are being distributed so effectively by the competitive markets, that it would be impossible to make any single person better off without harming some other person. Remember this phrase: "It would be impossible to make any single person better off without making some other person worse off." This is the ethical substance of microeconomic theory encapsulated in Pareto Optimality: produce the maximum economic benefits for society, recognizing the full personal and social costs of that production, and then broaden the receipt of those benefits if necessary by political, not economic, actions.

Pareto Optimality provides the ethical content of microeconomic theory; without this concept of social benefit, the theory deteriorates into a simple prescription for individual gain and corporate profit. With this concept, the theory becomes a means of achieving a social goal: maximum availability of goods and services produced at minimum cost. The theory requires that every business manager attempt to optimize profits. Consequently the decision rule that a microeconomist would propose for finding the proper balance between the economic and social performance of a business firm would be to always be truthful, honorable (i.e., observe contracts), and competitive, and always decide for the greater economic return. The question of this chapter is: Can we use this decision rule when faced with an ethical dilemma?

For many microeconomists, the concept of Pareto Optimality excludes any need to consider ethical dilemmas in management. This view is very direct and can be summarized very simply. "Ethics are not relevant in business, beyond the normal standards not to lie, cheat, or steal. All that is necessary is to maintain price-competitive markets and recognize the full costs of production in those prices, and then the market system will ensure that scarce resources are used to optimally satisfy consumer needs. A firm that is optimally satisfying consumer needs, to the limit of the available resources, is operating most efficiently and most profitably. Consequently, business managers should act to maximize profits, while following legal requirements of noncollusion and equal opportunity and adhering to personal standards of truthfulness and honesty. Profit maximization leads automatically from the satisfaction of individual consumer wants to the generation of maximum social benefits. Profit maximization is the only moral standard needed for management."

Is this summary an overstatement of the microeconomic view of ethics and management? Probably not. The belief that profit maximization leads inexorably to the well-being of society is a central tenet of economic theory and has been stated very succinctly and very clearly by both James McKie of the Brookings Institution and Milton Friedman of the University of Chicago:

> The primary goal and motivating force for business organizations is profit. The firm attempts to make as large a profit as it can, thereby maintaining its efficiency and taking advantage of available opportunities to innovate and contribute to growth. Profits are kept to reasonable or appropriate levels by market competition, which leads the firm pursuing its own self-interest to an end that is not part of its conscious intention: enhancement of the public welfare.[1]

* * * * *

> The view has been gaining widespread acceptance that corporate officials . . . have a "social responsibility" that goes beyond serving the interest of their stockholders or their members. This view shows a fundamental misconception of the character and nature of a free economy. In such an economy, there is one and only one social responsibility of business—to use its resources and engage in activities designed to increase its profits, so long as it stays within the rules of the game, which is to say, engages in open and free competition, without deception or fraud. . . . Few trends could so thoroughly undermine the very foundations of our free society as the acceptance by corporate officials of a social responsibility other than to make as much money for their stockholders as possible.[2]

The statement by Milton Friedman was expanded in an article, "The Social Responsibility of Business Is to Increase Its Profits,"[3] which often is assigned for students at business schools in classes on business economics or business and society. It is a frustrating article to read and then to discuss in class because it never makes clear the theoretical basis of Pareto Optimality; Professor Friedman assumes that the readers recognize and understand that basis of his contention.

THE MORAL PROBLEMS IN MICROECONOMIC THEORY

What is your opinion? Can we accept the microeconomic premise that profit optimization leads directly to maximum social benefits? The response of people trained in other disciplines is often much more pragmatic than theoretical, and it too can be summarized very simply: "Yes, we know the theory, but look at where the blind pursuit of profit has led us: foreign bribes, environmental problems, unsafe products, closed plants, and injured workers. We need something more than profit to measure our obligations to society." This view, I think, has been most sensibly expressed by Manuel Velasquez of the University of Santa Clara:

> . . . some have argued that in perfectly competitive free markets the pursuit of profit will by itself ensure that the members of society are served in the most socially beneficial ways. For, in order to be profitable, each firm has to produce only what the members of society want and has to do this by the most efficient means available. The members of society will benefit most, then, if managers do not impose their own values on a business but instead devote themselves to the single-minded pursuit of profit, and thereby devote themselves to producing efficiently what the members of society themselves value.
>
> Arguments of this sort conceal a number of assumptions. . . . First, most industrial markets are not "perfectly competitive" as the argument assumes, and to the extent that firms do not have to compete they can maximize profits in spite of inefficient production. Second, the argument assumes that any steps taken to increase profits will necessarily be socially beneficial, when in fact several ways of increasing profits actually injure society: allowing harmful pollution to go uncontrolled, deceptive advertising, concealing product hazards, fraud, bribery, tax evasion, price-fixing, and so on. Third, the argument assumes that by producing whatever the buying public wants (or values) firms are producing what all the members of society want, when in fact the wants of large segments of society (the poor and the disadvantaged) are not necessarily met because they cannot participate fully in the marketplace. . . .[4]

This pragmatic response, which can obviously be supported by many examples within our society, is not compelling to most economists. They believe that the issues cited—the lack of competitive markets, the presence of injurious practices, and the exclusion of some segments of society—are part of economic theory and would be prevented by its strict application. How would they be prevented? Here, it is necessary to provide an explanation of the extensive structure of economic theory and of the logical interrelationships that exist among the components in that structure: the individual consumers, product markets, producing firms, factor markets, factor owners, and public institutions. (The "factors" are the scarce resources of labor, capital, and material used in the production of goods and services.) Doubtless an explanation of this structure and these interrelationships will be dull for those with a good grasp of microeconomic theory, and trying for all others, but this explanation is necessary to deal with the ethical problems in the theory on a meaningful basis. If you truly are bored with microeconomic theory and willing to accept the rationality of the structure, skip ahead to page 48 and dive directly into the ethical claims of the theory.

THE BASIC STRUCTURE OF MICROECONOMIC THEORY

Microeconomic theory is complex. Perhaps, to make this brief explanation more comprehensible, it would be well to start with an overall summary. The focus of the theory, as stated previously, is the efficient utilization of scarce resources to maximize the production of wanted goods and services. The mechanism of the theory is the market structure: each firm is located between a "factor" market for the input factors of production (labor, material, and capital) and a "product" market for the output goods and services. The demand for each good or service is aggregated from the preference functions of individual consumers, who act to maximize their satisfactions from a limited mix of products. The supply of each good or service is aggregated from the production schedules of individual firms, which act to balance their marginal revenues and marginal costs at a limited level of capacity. The production of goods and services creates derived demands for the input factors of labor, material, and capital. These factors are substitutable—can be interchanged—so the derived demands vary with the costs. These costs, of course, reflect the constrained supplies in the different factor markets. A firm attempting to minimize costs and maximize revenues will therefore use the most available resources to produce the most needed products, generating not only the greatest profits for itself but the greatest benefits for society. The components of the theory, and the relationships among these components, which together produce corporate profits and social benefits, may be more understandable in graphic form, as shown in Exhibit 2–1.

EXHIBIT 2–1 _____

Graphic Summary of Microeconomic Theory

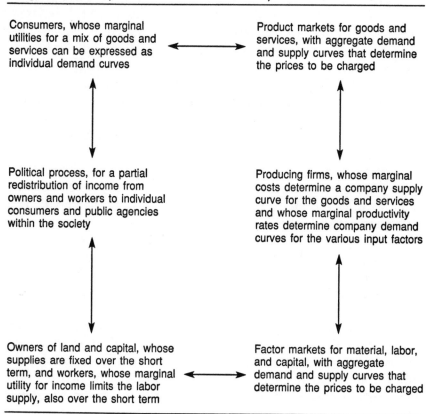

Consumers, whose marginal utilities for a mix of goods and services can be expressed as individual demand curves

Product markets for goods and services, with aggregate demand and supply curves that determine the prices to be charged

Political process, for a partial redistribution of income from owners and workers to individual consumers and public agencies within the society

Producing firms, whose marginal costs determine a company supply curve for the goods and services and whose marginal productivity rates determine company demand curves for the various input factors

Owners of land and capital, whose supplies are fixed over the short term, and workers, whose marginal utility for income limits the labor supply, also over the short term

Factor markets for material, labor, and capital, with aggregate demand and supply curves that determine the prices to be charged

Now it is necessary to work through the theory in somewhat greater detail to indicate the inclusion of ethical concepts and to be able to discuss the ethical problems that are integral with it.

Individual Consumers

Each consumer has a slightly different set of preferences for the various goods and services that are available, and these preferences can be expressed as "utilities," or quantitative measures of the usefulness of a given product or service to a specific consumer. The "marginal utility," or extra usefulness, of one additional unit of that product or service to that customer tends to decline, for eventually the person will have a surfeit of the good. The price that the person is willing to pay for the good also declines along with marginal utility or degree of surfeit. Price relative to the number of units that will be purchased by a given person at a given time forms the individual demand curve (see Exhibit 2–2).

Price can also be used to compare the relative usefulness of different goods and services to an individual. It can be expected that a person selecting a mix of products will choose an assortment of goods and services such that marginal utility per monetary unit would be equal for all the items at a given level of spending for this individual. Each good would be demanded up to the point where the marginal utility per dollar would be exactly the same as the marginal utility per dollar for any other good. If a customer had a higher marginal utility relative to price for any particular good, he or she would doubtless substitute more of that good for some of the others to achieve a better balance among his or her preferences. The final balance or mix, where the marginal utilities per monetary unit are equal for all products and services, can be termed the point of equilibrium for that customer.

The concept of consumer equilibrium is an important element in the structure of the economic condition termed Pareto Optimality. A customer with balanced marginal utilities per monetary unit for all available goods and services cannot be made better off at his or her level of spending, according to his or her standards of preference. The customer may buy hamburgers, french fries,

EXHIBIT 2–2
Marginal Utility Curve

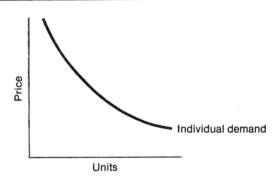

and beer, and we may think that he or she should be buying fish, fresh vegetables, and fruit, but that person is satisfying his or her standards, not our own, and they are being satisfied up to the limits of his or her ceiling on expenditures. Consequently, that person cannot be made better off without an increase in disposable income. Now, let us look at the determination of the level of disposable income in microeconomic theory. This is more complex than the determination of the mix of desired purchases, but the logical structure can be followed through the product markets, the producing firms, the factor markets, the private owners of those factors, and the public processes for redistribution of factor income.

Product Markets

A product market consists of all the customers for a given good or service, together with all the producing firms that supply that good or service. The individual demand curves of all the customers can be aggregated to form a market demand curve. The market demand curve reflects the total demand for a good or service, relative to price, and it generally slopes downward, indicating increased potential purchases at the lower price levels. Crossing this market demand curve is a market supply curve that portrays the total available supply, again relative to price. The market supply curve generally slopes upward, for the higher the price, the more units in total most companies can be expected to manufacture, until they reach a short-term limit of capacity. The market price, of course, is set at the intersection of the curves representing aggregate demand and aggregate supply (see Exhibit 2–3).

Producing Firms

The aggregate supply curve, the "other half" of each product market, is formed by adding together the individual supply curves of all the producers. These individual supply curves are generated by the cost structures of the producing firms at different levels of production, while the actual level of production is determined by a comparison of "marginal revenues" and "marginal costs." The marginal revenue of a producing firm is the extra

EXHIBIT 2–3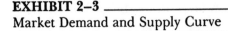
Market Demand and Supply Curve

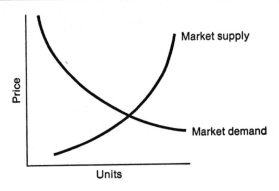

revenue that the firm would receive by selling one additional unit of the good or service. To sell that additional unit in a fully price-competitive market, it is necessary to move down the aggregate demand curve to a slightly lower price level. To sell that additional unit in a non-price-competitive market, it is necessary to spend greater amounts on advertising and promotion to differentiate the product from those manufactured by other firms. Under either alternative, the marginal revenue from selling the last unit will be less than the average revenue from selling all other units; marginal revenues inevitably decrease with volume.

The marginal cost of the producing firm is the obverse of the marginal revenue. Marginal cost is the extra expense that the firm would incur by producing one additional unit of the product or service. Marginal costs initially decline with volume due to economies of scale and learning curve effects, but they eventually rise due to diminishing returns as the physical capacity of the plant is approached. The rising portion of the marginal cost curve forms the supply curve of the firm; it represents the number of units that the firm should produce and supply to the market at each price level (see Exhibit 2–4).

The producing firm achieves equilibrium when marginal costs are equal to marginal revenues. At the intersection of the marginal cost and marginal revenue curves, the profits of the firm are maximized. The firm can increase profits only by improving its technology; this would change the marginal costs and consequently the supply curve. However, over the long term, all firms

EXHIBIT 2–4 _____
Marginal Cost Curve

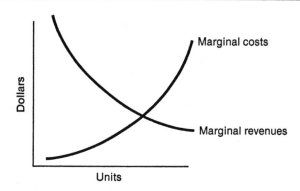

would adopt the new technology and achieve the same cost structure. Production equilibrium would be reestablished at the new intersections of the marginal cost and marginal revenue curves for all firms within the industry.

All the costs of production have to be included in computing the marginal cost curve for a firm. This is the second of the ethical constructs in microeconomic theory, along with the individual selection of goods and services according to private preference standards, or "utilities." The internal personal costs (e.g., hazardous working conditions) and the external social costs (e.g., harmful environmental discharges) have to be computed, so that customers pay the full costs of production. The technology, of course, can be changed to improve working conditions and reduce environmental discharges, and this should be done to bring marginal costs down to marginal revenues at a new, nonhazardous and nonpolluting equilibrium, but it is an essential element in microeconomic theory that product-market prices reflect the *full* costs of production.

Factor Markets

The technology of the producing firm determines the maximum output of goods and services that can be achieved for a given mix of input factors. The input factors of production are land (an apparently obsolete term that instead refers to all of the basic raw materials), labor, and capital. Charges for the input factors are rents for the land and other basic resources, wages for the labor, and interest for the capital. These charges are interdependent because the factors are interrelated; that is, one factor may be substituted for others in the production function. The relationships among these input factors, and the amount of one that would have to be used to substitute for another, are determined by the technology of the production function and by the "marginal productivity" of each factor for a given technology. The marginal productivity of a factor of production is the additional output generated by adding one more unit of that factor while keeping all others constant. For example, it is possible to add one additional worker to a production line without changing the capital investments in the line and the material components of the product; there should be an increase in the physical output of that production line, and that increase, measured in units or portions of units, would be the marginal productivity of that worker. To maximize profits, a company should increase the use of each factor of production until the value of its marginal product (the increase in unit output, or productivity, times the value of those units) equals the cost of the input factor.

Factor Owners

The aggregate demand for each factor of production is equal to the production of that factor used in the production function of each firm times the output of those functions supplied to meet the product market demand. The demand for each factor of production is therefore "derived" from the primary markets for goods and services. The aggregate supply of each factor of production is limited. Over the long term, stocks of the basic materials may be expanded by bringing into production marginal agricultural lands, oilfields, and ore mines, and the reserves of investment capital may be increased by raising the rate of capital formation. Over the short term, however, the supply amounts are fixed. Aggregate supplies of labor are also limited, though for a different cause: each worker has a marginal utility for income that decreases and becomes negative as his or her desire for greater leisure exceeds his or her preference for further work. This negative utility function creates a "backward sloping" supply curve for labor and sharply limits the amounts available at the higher wage rates. The price system in the different factor markets, therefore, ensures that the limited factors of production will be used in the most economically effective manner to produce the goods and services to be sold in the product markets, and that the rents, wages, and interest paid for these factors will reflect both the productivity of the factor and the derived demand of the goods (see Exhibit 2–5).

Political Processes

The owners of the factors of production, within a capitalistic society, are also the customers for the products and services generated by the production functions at the various firms. The owners receive the rents, the wages, and the interest payments for the use of their resources and then purchase the goods and services they want, following their personal preferences or utilities. There is a political process for the redistribution of the rents, wages, and interest payments, through both tax provisions and welfare allocations, so that no individual or group is unable to participate in the product markets for the various goods and services. This political process is the third ethical construct in microeconomic theory; it ensures that the distribution of the revenues for material, capital, and labor will be "equitable," following a democratically determined definition of equity.

EXHIBIT 2–5
Factor Supply Curves

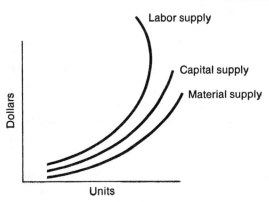

THE MORAL CLAIMS OF MICROECONOMIC THEORY

Now that there is a common understanding of the basic structure of microeconomic theory, or the logical system of relationships among individual customers, product markets, producing firms, factor markets, resource owners, and political processes, it is possible to look at the claims of that theory relative to the social welfare. There are five explicit assertions:

1. The price mechanisms of the factor markets allocate the scarce resources of society to their most effective uses. The marginal productivity of each factor together with the cost (reflecting supply versus demand) determines the relative usage of the factors by the producing firms. At factor equilibrium, it would be impossible to expand total production without an increase in resource supply.

2. The production functions of the producing firms convert the limited input factors into wanted output goods and services by the most effective methods (process technologies) and at the most efficient rates (output amounts). A firm's technology and capacity are long-term decisions, while the operating rate is a short-term choice, but all are based upon the balance between marginal revenues and marginal costs. Internal personal harms and external social damages are included in the marginal costs. At process equilibrium, it would be impossible to convert resources into products more efficiently and with less personal harm or social damage without an advance in technology.

3. The price mechanisms of the product markets distribute the wanted goods and services of society to their most effective uses. The marginal utilities of each customer together with the prices (again reflecting supply versus demand) for the various products determine the relative consumption of the goods and services. At market equilibrium, it would be impossible to improve consumer satisfaction without an increase in personal income.

4. The political processes of the national society determine the personal income of each consumer through democratic means. The income may be distributed according to ownership of the factors of production, or according to an individual's need, effort, contribution, or competence. Distribution of the benefits of the economic system is a political, not an economic, process.

5. The economic system, provided the managers of the producing firms act to maximize profits, the customers for the goods and services act to maximize satisfactions, and the owners of the resources act to maximize revenues, will operate efficiently, producing the greatest output of wanted goods and services for the least input of scarce labor, capital, and material. If the revenues to the owners of the factors of production are equitably redistributed to the customers of the producing firms through a democratic decision process, it would be impossible to improve the life of any member of the system without harming the life of another member, because the system would have reached Pareto Optimality. Consequently, the social responsibility of the managers of the producing firms is to maximize profits and leave the redistribution of economic benefits to the political process.

PRAGMATIC OBJECTIONS TO MICROECONOMIC THEORY

The usual objections to microeconomic theory are pragmatic in nature, based upon very obvious problems in our national society, and they generally include the three issues discussed by Professor Velasquez in the statement quoted earlier in this chapter:

1. The exclusion of segments of society. It is alleged that the minorities and the poor, because they lack ownership of any of the factors of production beyond their unskilled labor, receive inadequate income to participate in the product markets and consequently cannot maximize their own satisfactions in any meaningful way. The microeconomic response is quite obvious. "We grant you that this happens, but it is the fault of the political process and not of the economic system. You develop logically attractive political decision rules for the more equitable division of the benefits, and we will work to economically maximize the production of those benefits within market and resource constraints.

2. The presence of injurious practices. It is also alleged that managers of productive firms, because of an excessive concern with maximizing profits, have permitted or even encouraged some practices that are injurious to some members of society, through workplace dangers or environmental pollution, or that are destructive to the market system, through purchase bribes or employment discrimination. Here, the response of most economists would be that these problems occur, but that they would not occur under the strict application of the theory. Let us look at a number of specific problems and the theoretical solutions:

Purchase Bribes. Personal payments to influence purchase decisions are evidently common overseas, and not unknown within the United States. In an efficient market, however, bribes would be futile; they would raise the cost function by an amount equivalent to the payment, so that nonbribing competitors would have an obvious price advantage. The microeconomic response is obvious: insist that purchase decisions be open and subject to public comparison of the bids, to ensure the selection of the lowest-priced proposal to supply needed goods and services. The lowest-priced proposal would necessarily come from a nonbribing competitor.

Process Pollutants. Many industrial processes result in toxic residues and inert materials as by-products, which are now either discharged as air or water pollutants or buried as liquid or solid wastes. The toxic by-products have an obvious social cost, both immediate and long term. The microeconomic response has been clearly stated many times: companies should recognize these costs that are external to the productive process and include them in the pricing function. It might be expected, were these external costs accurately computed, that investments in proper disposal equipment would become clearly beneficial for the firm, or if they were fully included in the price, the product would become overly expensive for the customer; under either alternative, the amount of pollution would be substantially reduced.

Workplace Hazards. It would appear that many of the mechanical hazards of industrial processing have been eliminated; 40 years of state and federal labor laws have removed the unprotected belts, open gearing, and nonshielded presses. Chemical risks still remain, however, and psychological problems will probably always be a part of mass manufacturing, due to the repetitive nature of the tasks and the time constraints of the process. The microeconomic response to workplace hazards is similar to that for process pollutants: the nonfactor costs of production should be computed and added to the price. Certainly, if the market is to operate efficiently to allocate resources within the society, customers have to pay the full costs of production, not partial costs subsidized by the physical or mental health of the workers.

Product Dangers. The press has recently reported numerous instances of unsafe products, particularly in the automobile industry. Gas tanks poorly located, radial tires poorly fabricated, and automatic transmissions poorly designed have all been mentioned, together with such nonautomotive products as hair dryers (containing asbestos), teddy bears (containing sharp objects), and packaged foods (containing nonnutrients). I think it safe to assume that the microeconomic response would be that a product offered for sale within a competitive market should perform the function for which it was designed, and that many of the reported failures and hazards come from decisions to differentiate products in slight or artificial ways to avoid the discipline of price competition. Whatever the cause of product failure and hazards, the costs of improper design are now being charged back against the manufacturing firms through liability suits and jury awards, and it can be assumed that product safety will soon be improved as a result of objective economic analysis.

Minority Employment. Racial or sexual discrimination in employment, in an efficient labor market, would be self-defeating; a work force limited to young or middle-aged white males would raise the cost of labor in the productive function and provide the nondiscriminating employer with a cost advantage. It is assumed, in economic analysis, that all groups are equal in performance capabilities. Training might be needed to justify that assumption, but the microeconomic response would be that training to correct social injustices should be provided as a public investment. Cost-benefit analysis would assuredly show an economic return on that investment, as well as a social gain.

3. The absence of competitive markets. Last, it is often claimed that the product markets for consumer goods and services are not price competitive because of oligopolistic practices among the producing firms serving those markets. Companies have become much larger recently, doubtless due to economies of scale in production and distribution, while products have become more "differentiated," marked by only slight or imagined distinctions in performance and design but supported by excessive advertising. The dominance of large firms in each market, and the inability of customers to judge the relative worth of products in those markets, is said to lead toward "administered" rather than competitive prices. Administered pricing, where the price level is set by the company to provide a set return above costs without reference to either supply or demand, of course destroys the efficiency of the market. The economic response, however, is very simple. "Oh, we grant you that market structures are not truly competitive, and that market processes are not actually efficient under current conditions. However, no one is advocating limited competition or inadequate information. Public policy changes to restrict competitor size and to ensure consumer information are needed to reestablish the discipline of the market."

THEORETIC OBJECTIONS TO MICROECONOMIC THEORY

Microeconomic theory is awesomely complete. There are few operating decisions in business to which it could not be applied—from hiring workers, purchasing supplies, and borrowing money to selecting technologies, establishing capacities, and setting prices. Likewise, there are few ethical problems to which microeconomic theory is not applicable, whether purchase bribes, process pollutants, workplace hazards, product dangers, or racial discrimination. It is very difficult to say, "Here is a managerial decision or action with definite ethical implications that is not included in the theory."

Microeconomic theory is also enviably unified. All the managerial decisions and actions work together, through a system of explicit relationships, to create a socially desirable goal: maximum output of the wanted goods and services at a minimum input of the scarce material, capital, and labor. It is very difficult to say, "Here is a managerial decision or action following microeconomic theory that does not lead to a socially beneficial outcome."

Where does this discussion lead us? Are we forced to accept microeconomic theory as an ethical system of belief for business management because of the complete and unified nature of the paradigm? Should we always act to maximize profits, as long as we are truthful, honest, and competitive, and use the concept of Pareto Optimality as the substitute for our ethical concerns? Or, is there a theoretic problem with that paradigm? Most noneconomists are intuitively distressed by the proposal that business managers have no moral responsibilities to other members of society, outside of fiduciary duties to a small circle of owners, and that managers also are governed by no moral requirements of behavior beyond adhering to personal standards of honesty and truthfulness, observing legal statutes for contracts and against collusion, and computing accurate costs for personal harms and social dangers. Why is this distressing, and what are the arguments against the microeconomic model that can be expressed on a theoretic rather than a pragmatic or intuitive basis? There are two major arguments; one pertains to the assumptions about human nature and the second centers on the assumptions about human worth that are part of microeconomic theory.

1. Assumptions about the nature of human beings. The microeconomic model is utilitarian (see Chapter 4 for a definition of utilitarianism, a philosophic system that has often been roughly translated as "the greatest good for the greatest number"). It takes the position that the ultimate end is the greatest general good, and it defines that good as the maximum benefits of consumer products and services at the minimum costs of labor, capital, and material. The problem, as with all utilitarian theories, is that the distribution of the benefits and the imposition of the costs may be unjust. Consequently, it is necessary to add a political process to the economic paradigm to ensure justice in the distribution of benefits and the imposition of costs. But, "justice" is defined in the theory as a democratically determined pattern of distribution and imposition; this pattern does not follow a rule such as, to each person equally, or to each according to his or her need, to his or her effort, to his or her contribution, to his or her competence, or even to his or her ownership of the factors of production. Instead, the pattern varies with the collective opinions of the members of society. This requires all members of society to be actively concerned with the charitable distribution of social benefits and imposition of social costs *at the same time* as they are actively concerned with the personal maximization of material goods and services in the product markets and of financial wages, rents, and interest payments in the factor markets, solely for themselves. I think that we can safely say that human nature exhibits both selfish and generous traits, and we can doubtless go further and

accept that human beings can perform selfish and then generous acts alternately, but it would seem an extreme assumption to believe that people can concurrently be generously attentive to others in all political decisions and selfishly attentive to themselves in all economic activities, and never confuse the two roles. The microeconomic model would appear to be based upon an exceedingly complex and unlikely view of the nature of human beings.

2. Assumptions about the value of human beings. The microeconomic model is impersonal, for it requires that everyone be treated as a means to an end and not as an end in himself or herself. Customers for goods and services are people who maximize material satisfactions as a means of determining product-demand curves. Owners of land, capital, and labor are people who maximize financial revenues as a means of determining factor-supply curves. Company managers are people who maximize corporate profits as a means of balancing market demand and factor supply. No one acts as an individual human being, pursuing personal goals worthy of consideration and respect. This denial of worth can be seen particularly clearly in the position of the manager of the firm, who must act solely as an agent for the financial interests of the stockholders. What does this do to self-esteem and to self-respect? How can people live worthwhile lives when always being treated as a means to other people's ends—or, perhaps even worse, when always treating others as means to their own ends—even though the society as an economic system may have achieved Pareto Optimality? The microeconomic model would appear to be based upon an exceedingly low view of the worth of human beings.

Where does this discussion of managerial ethics and microeconomic theory lead us? There would seem to be two major conclusions. If we look at microeconomic theory as a structured pattern of relationships explaining the optimal uses of scarce material, capital, and labor to produce the optimal numbers of consumer goods and services, then it is a logically complete and intellectually satisfying view of the world. But, if we look at microeconomic theory as an ethical system of belief, explaining our responsibility to others within the company and within the society—to employees, customers, suppliers, distributors, and residents of the local area

—then it simply falls apart because of the unlikely assumptions about human nature and human worth. We are going to have to look elsewhere for a means of reaching decisions when confronted with an ethical dilemma, with a conflict between the economic performance and the social performance of a business firm. We are going to have to look either to the rule of law or to the doctrines of normative philosophy to determine what is "right" and "just" and "proper."

Notes

1. James McKie, *Changing Views, Social Responsibility and the Business Predicament* (Washington, D.C.: Brookings Institution, 1974), p. 19.

2. Milton Friedman, *Capitalism and Freedom* (Chicago: University of Chicago Press, 1962), p. 133.

3. *New York Times Magazine*, September 13, 1970, p. 32f.

4. Manuel Velasquez, *Business Ethics: Concepts and Causes* (New York: Prentice-Hall, 1982), pp. 17-18.

CASES

When Is It Permissible to Pay a Bribe?

"Bribe" in the context of this series of examples of cash or benefit payments made to influence decisions is an overstatement. A bribe technically is an *illegal* cash or benefit payment made to influence the decision of an individual or a group, and none of the following examples is illegal under current U.S. law.

These payments of cash or benefits may not be illegal under current U.S. law, but that does not automatically mean that they are right. Some of these payments are uncommon, and apparently many people do object to them. "I know that sort of thing happens occasionally in our industry, but we don't do it" is a typical comment. Others of the payments are so common that they are considered to be accepted practices. "Everybody does it, and I for one see nothing wrong with it" is often the explanation here.

Decide which of the following *legal* cash or benefit payments are "right" and which are "wrong" in your opinion. And, be prepared to say why you think that they are "right" or "wrong":

1. Many large U.S. manufacturers now operate abroad in sections of the world where cash payments to government officials in return for purchase contracts, import privileges, or tax concessions may be illegal under local law but are still either acknowledged or tolerated by local custom. The U.S. firms are forbidden to make those payments under terms of the Foreign Corrupt Practices Act. European and Japanese companies are not under similar constraints, and it is said that their ability to follow those local customs has enabled them to receive many of the contracts, privileges, and concessions that formerly went to the U.S. firms. It is also now said that many of the U.S. firms have adopted the practice of hiring local consultants who claim to be able to obtain the contracts, privileges, and concessions legitimately. The invoices from the local consultants, however, are generally 20 percent above the amounts of the requested bribes, which has led to the suspicion that the consultants are simply paying the bribes in lieu of the U.S. firms. Is it permissible to hire those consultants?

2. It is illegal within the United States to make direct cash payments to government officials, except to members of the legislative branches at the national and state levels where the payments are often considered to be honoraria in return for speeches at conventions or attendance at meetings. It is not illegal, however, to provide noncash benefits to members of the executive branches, again at the national and state levels. For example, almost all of the large defense contractors maintain hunting lodges along the Maryland shore (hunting for ducks and geese) and in South Carolina (hunting for quail, woodcock, or wood doves). It is felt that many of the senior officers in the military like to hunt and that inviting them to participate, along with company officials, in the often rustic conditions of a hunting lodge is an inexpensive but effective means of "building future relationships."

3. A combination of cash payments and noncash benefits may be provided by American companies to members of the legislative branches at both national and state levels. State legislators are often paid to attend dinners or other meetings—generally within the capital city and not at a vacation resort—at which possible changes in state laws are discussed. For example, 3M Corporation admitted in August 1988, that it had paid an honorarium of $250 each to members of the Michigan state legislature to attend an evening meeting to discuss a bill that would mandate reflectorized license plates. 3M makes the special paint required for reflectorized license plates.

4. A combination of cash payments and noncash benefits may also be provided by American companies to professionals in such fields as law or medicine. It is felt to be difficult for salespeople to meet with active lawyers or physicians in their offices, due to their time constraints, and so all-expense-paid trips to a central meeting place at a pleasant vacation resort are frequently arranged. For example, Merck and Company admitted in August 1988, that it made a practice of offering all-expense-paid weekend trips to physicians and their spouses to the Monterey Peninsula in California to hear company scientists discuss research advances in prescription drugs. The all-expense-paid trips included first-class airfares, hotel accommodations, meals at the Lodge (a four-star resort), and guest memberships at the Pebble Beach Golf Club (a championship course directly on the Pacific Ocean). Merck, of course, manufactures and markets prescription drugs.

5. Cash payments and noncash benefits do not necessarily go only to individuals, nor do they necessarily stop at government officials, business executives, attorneys, and physicians. At some large universities, where the selection of the textbook for an introductory course will result in the sale of hundreds of copies, it is now common for publishers to be asked to contribute a portion of the profits from those sales to the department responsible for the selection to support research funding.

Class Assignment. Decide which of these actions are right and which are wrong. Follow your own opinion, but be prepared to support that opinion. Don't just give your answer and then stop; instead be ready to say why you think they are right or why you think they are wrong.

Financial Compensation for the Victims of Bhopal

On December 3, 1984, some 2,000 people were killed and 200,000 were injured when a cloud of poisonous methyl isocyanate gas was accidentally released from the Union Carbide Company plant in Bhopal, India. The methyl isocyanate was used to manufacture Sevin, a plant pesticide that was distributed widely throughout India for use on that country's corn, rice, soybean, cotton, and alfalfa crops. It was said that the use of Sevin increased the harvest of the food crops by over 10 percent, enough to feed 70 million people.

The accident apparently occurred when between 120 and 240 gallons of water were introduced into a tank containing 90,000 pounds of methyl isocyanate.[1] The tank also contained approximately 3,000 pounds of chloroform, which is used as a solvent in the manufacture of methyl isocyanate; the two chemicals should have been separated before storage, but that had not been done for some time in the operating process at Bhopal.

The water reacted exothermically (producing heat) with the chloroform, generating chlorine ions, which led to corrosion of the tank walls, and the iron oxide from the corrosion in turn reacted exothermically with the methyl isocyanate. The increase in heat and pressure was rapid but unnoticed because the pressure gauge on the tank had been inoperable for four months and the operators in the control room, monitoring a remote temperature gauge, were accustomed to higher-than-specified heat levels (25°C rather than the 0°C in the operating instructions) due to the continual presence of the chloroform and some water vapor in the tank. The refrigeration unit built to cool the storage tank had been disconnected six months previously. The "scrubber," a safety device to neutralize the methyl isocyanate with caustic soda, had been under repair since June. An operator, alarmed by the suddenly increasing temperature, attempted to cool the tank by spraying it with water, but by then the reaction was unstoppable, at a probable 200°C. The rupture disc (a steel plate in the line to prevent accidental operation of the safety valve) broke, the safety valve opened (just before, it is assumed, the tank would have burst), and over half the 45 tons of methyl isocyanate in storage were discharged into the air.

Following the accident, Union Carbide officials in the United States denied strongly that their firm was responsible for the tragedy. They made the following three statements in support of that position:

1. The Bhopal plant was 50.9 percent owned by the American firm, but the parent corporation had been able to exercise very little control. All managerial and technical personnel were citizens of India at the insistence of the Indian government. No Americans were permanently employed at the plant. Safety warnings from visiting American inspectors about the Sevin manufacturing process had been ignored.

2. Five automatic safety devices that had originally been installed as part of the Sevin manufacturing process had, by the time of the accident, been either replaced by manual safety methods to increase employment, shut down for repairs, or disconnected as part of a cost-reduction program. The automatic temperature and pressure warning signals had been removed soon after construction. The repairs on the automatic scrubber unit had extended over six months. The refrigeration unit had never been used to cool the tank and had been inoperable for over a year.

3. The Bhopal plant had been built in partnership with the Indian government to increase employment in that country. Union Carbide would have preferred to make Sevin in the United States and ship it to India for distribution and sale, because the insecticide could be made less expensively in the United States due to substantial economies of scale in the manufacturing process.

Warren Anderson, chairman of Union Carbide, stated that while he believed that the American company was not legally liable for the tragedy due to the three points above, it was still "morally" responsible, and he suggested that the firm should pay prompt financial compensation to those killed and injured in the accident.

Class Assignment. Assume that the question of legal liability for the accident at Bhopal never will be settled, due to differences in the law between the two countries and the difficulties of establishing jurisdiction. Assume, however, that the American company is morally responsible for the tragedy, as admitted by the chairman, because it was the majority owner and yet did not insist that the unsafe process be shut down. What factors would you consider in setting just financial compensation for each of the victims?

Note

1. Seven engineers and scientists from the Union Carbide Corporation were sent to Bhopal to assist in the safe disposal of the remaining methyl isocyanate at that site and to investigate the reasons for the accident. They were not permitted to interview operators of the Sevin process or to inspect the methyl isocyanate storage tank and related piping. They were permitted to obtain samples of the residues from the nearly ruptured tank; through experimentation they were able to replicate reactions that led to residues with the same chemical properties in the same proportions. The account, therefore, is a hypothesis for the tragedy, not a proven series of events.

The Leveraged Buyout of RJR Nabisco

On October 15, 1988, the stock of RJR Nabisco was selling at $56 per share. The company was a conglomerate, put together during the period 1978 to 1985 by means of mergers of R. J. Reynolds (cigarettes and other tobacco products), Standard Brands (coffee, tea, margarine, candy, wine, and liquor), the National Biscuit Company (cookies, crackers, and breakfast cereals), and Del Monte Corporation (canned goods).

On October 20, F. Ross Johnson, the chairman and chief executive officer of RJR Nabisco, announced an offer to "take the company private" at $75 per share. Taking the company private meant that RJR Nabisco, supported by the investment banking firm of Shearson Lehman Brothers, was offering to buy back from the existing shareholders all of the common stock of the company. The assets of the company were to be pledged as security for the bank loans and corporate bonds needed to pay for that common stock, in a process known as a "leveraged buyback." The company would then be "restructured," which meant that new common stock would be sold to the members of the management and the partners in the investment banking firm who had arranged the buyback. The new common stock would not be publicly traded on one of the stock exchanges but would be privately held by the investors. Consequently, the complete process was termed "taking a company private through a leveraged buyout or leveraged buyback."

How exactly does a "leveraged buyout" (an offer to purchase all of the stock by an outside group of "raiders") or a "leveraged buyback" (an offer to purchase all of the stock by an inside group of managers) work? It is easiest to explain the complete process as a series of steps:

1. The investor group, whether made up of outside raiders or inside managers, puts up approximately 10 percent of the purchase price in cash, using either their own resources or those of an investment bank. Investment banks have traditionally been willing to commit their capital to facilitate a buyout or buyback because they receive substantial fees for advising on the transaction, substantial commissions for the eventual sale of the corporate bonds, and a substantial portion of the equity of the "restructured" firm.

2. Then the investor group, relying on the assets of the company as collateral, borrows 30 to 40 percent of the purchase price from a syndicate of commercial banks. Commercial banks have traditionally been willing to commit their capital to finance a buyout or buyback becasue they hold allegedly secure collateral for the loan amounts and receive substantial fees for the loan commitments.

3. Finally, the investment bank, acting either by itself or as a member of a syndicate of other investment banks, raises the balance of 50 to 60 percent of the purchase price through the sale of high-risk "junk" bonds to savings and loan institutions, mutual bond funds, and investment pension trusts. The savings and loans, mutual funds, and investment trusts have traditionally been willing to invest their capital in these bonds because they receive much higher interest rates than could be obtained from more normal investments.

4. The existing stockholders—including arbitrageurs, who buy in anticipation of the price increase that almost inevitably follows a buyout or buyback offer—are paid the bid price of the stock. The stockholders are not forced to sell. They "tender" their stock, or promise to make it available in the event that the buyback or buyout is completed. The buyback or buyout is completed when a substantial majority of the stockholders (the actual percentage required by law varies from state to state) have tendered their shares.

5. After the buyout or buyback is completed, selected portions of the company are sold in order to repay the bank loans (known as "bridge" loans due to the short amount of time they are expected to be in effect). The company is then owned by the members of the investor group and the partners of the investment bank, and financed by the junk bonds. The high interest charges of the junk bonds continue, of course, and usually no dividends are paid on the common stock in order to use all of the available cash flow to service the debt and repay the bonds. The available cash flow is usually increased by eliminating the luxuries and perks of management, and frequently, though not inevitably, by cutting employment, reducing R&D, closing plants, and halting capital improvements. Once the junk bonds have been repaid, the company can be "taken public" again through a public issuance and sale of the stock on one of the major stock exchanges. Very large profits can be made by the members of the investor group and the partners of the investment bank when (and if) the company can be successfully taken public.

The actual buyout or buyback process is usually not as direct, simple, or straightforward as has been described. Once the first offer has been made, the company is considered to be "in play." Other investor groups make higher offers. Other investment banks propose different terms. Arbitrageurs and private investors buy and sell legally on the public rumors (or illegally on the "inside" information) of higher bids and/or unavailable financing. "Unavailable financing," of course, means that a prior bid that had been considered legitimate must be taken off the market, and the next lower bid becomes the probable price for the buyout or buyback.

In the particular case of RJR Nabisco, Ross Johnson made the initial offer of $75 per share on October 20, 1988. Mr. Johnson said that despite the best efforts of his management team, the price of the stock had remained depressed at $56 per share for a number of years, and he wanted to "increase value for the shareholders."

On October 24, Kohlberg Kravis Roberts (a private banking firm and "buyout" specialist) bid $90 per share. They said that the stock of RJR Nabisco was obviously worth much more than the $75 per share offered by Mr. Johnson and questioned his motives in making the original offer at "such an unrealistic figure."

On November 4, Mr. Johnson and Shearson Lehman Brothers increased their bid to $92 per share. They claimed, in making the new offer, that Kohlberg Kravis Roberts wanted only to break up the company (i.e., divide it into its basic product divisions of tobacco, coffee, tea, etc.) and sell off those pieces to the highest bidder, which often meant a foreign firm wishing to enter the U.S. market. Mr. Johnson, on the other hand, said that only poorly performing divisions would be sold under his restructuring plan.

On November 5, a spokesperson for Kohlberg Kravis Roberts released to the press an internal document from RJR Nabisco that detailed the agreement between that company and Shearson Lehman Brothers. It was not explained how Kohlberg Kravis Roberts had obtained the document.

The document stated that Ross Johnson and six to nine other executives (the other executives were not named, and it was unclear why the number might vary) would receive 8.5 percent of the stock in the new company at the successful completion of the buyback. The balance of the stock was to go to the partners at Shearson Lehman Brothers and to a series of wealthy private investors and university endowment funds that were providing the original 10 percent of the purchase price, and (in small amounts, as a "sweetener") to some of the savings and loans, mutual funds, and pension trusts that were expected to purchase the junk bonds.

The stock percentage allocated to Mr. Johnson and his fellow executives was to increase to 20 percent, provided certain conditions were met. These conditions involved the sale of over 50 percent of the divisions of the company, both those that were classified as poorly performing and others that were operating profitably, by certain times and at certain figures, in order to rapidly repay all of the bridge loans and some of the junk bonds.

The 8.5 percent of the stock in the company allocated to Mr. Johnson and his fellow executives was to be purchased for $20 million in total (not $20 million from each executive). The company was to provide an interest-free loan of $20 million to the group in order to facilitate that purchase. The additional stock, if the certain conditions were met, was to be provided as a "bonus."

The amounts of stock that were to go to the Shearson Lehman Brothers partners, wealthy private investors, university endowment funds, and junk bond purchasers were large and apparently promised a return of 35 percent to 50 percent per year on their investments, but these amounts and returns were common in leveraged buyouts and buybacks and raised no concerns among members of the financial community.

The amounts of stock that were to go to Mr. Johnson and the six to nine other executives were considered to be unprecedented by people within the financial community. If RJR Nabisco were valued at the most recent offer of $92 per share for all of the stock in the firm, then the company, as it currently existed, was worth $22 billion. Granted, the stock to be issued to Mr. Johnson and the small group of other executives would be in the restructured firm after the issuance of junk bonds, but it had to be assumed that the $92 bid price represented Mr. Johnson's accurate valuation of the worth of the company's assets. Mr. Johnson and the six to nine other executives were to be given stock worth $1.87 billion and were required to invest only $20 million in the form of a non-interest-paying loan from the company. If the certain conditions of the buyback were met, that small group would receive additional stock worth $2.53 billion as a bonus, for a total of $4.4 billion. Members of Congress and representatives of the media expressed both shock and outrage.

On November 7, a spokesperson for Frostman Little, a private investment bank, said that the very large amounts of capital being used to compensate members of management indicated that the value being placed upon RJR Nabisco was still too low, and announced a new offer of $97 per share. Frostman Little, a relatively small investment bank, said that it was financially supported by Procter & Gamble, Castle & Cook, and Ralston Purina, all large manufacturers and marketers of packaged consumer goods and food products. It seemed obvious to members of the financial community that arrangements had already been made by Frostman Little for the purchase of the nontobacco divisions of RJR Nabisco by those manufacturers and marketers, and that consequently the $97 bid approached an accurate valuation for the firm.

On November 16, Ross Johnson and Shearson Lehman Brothers raised their bid to $100 per share and announced that the package of compensation for the senior executives has been misunderstood and was being rescinded. It was not stated exactly what compensation arrangements would be made to replace that original package. It was known that Kohlberg Kravis Roberts was planning to rebid before the final deadline of November 23, and it was thought that Frostman Little might also do so.

Ross Johnson and the partners at Shearson Lehman Brothers realized that they would have to submit another bid, higher than their current offer of $100 per share, to defeat the other contestants. They had invited Salomon Brothers, a very large investment banking firm with expertise in selling junk bonds, to participate in the bidding process. The participants in that process began to gather shortly after 9:00 on the morning of November 23 to set the price and terms of the final bid, which was due at the offices of Skadden Arps (attorneys for RJR Nabisco) at 5:00 that afternoon.

The problem was to select a number, above $100 per share, that would just barely exceed the final bids from the other competitors. Those final bids, of course, were unknown. Consequently, the selection process became a guessing game. No one wanted to name a specific figure and become personally responsible for the eventual success or failure of the largest buyout in the history of the merger movement. Everyone wanted someone else to name that figure and assume that responsibility.

For six hours, interrupted by telephone calls to and from friends, informants, and experts, the investment bankers and company executives alternately considered and then avoided talking about the size of the final bid in an aura of increasing urgency and concern. *The Wall Street Journal*[1] reported that these supposed sophisticated discussions of financial market economics were punctuated with cries of "Let's get on with it," "Christ, we need a goddamn number," "If you don't make up your minds soon, we'll have no bid at all," and "Can you believe this? I can't believe that this is happening."

Just after three o'clock a number was selected, apparently at random (no one ever claimed responsibility). The number was $114 per share. That figure had to be entered into the formal bid, a six-inch-thick package of cash flows, proforma statements, repayment schedules, loan guarantees, and interest rates, all of which were influenced by this final price for the company. Across Manhattan, at commercial banks, law offices, and accounting firms, the numbers were computed and telephoned or faxed to the 87th floor office of Shearson Lehman Brothers where the bid package was being assembled. At 4:20 four attorneys were ordered into a cab with the incomplete bid package and a portable telephone; they were to write in final numbers during the trip to the law offices of Skadden Arps where the bid was due precisely at 5:00.

Traffic in Manhattan is never light and this was a Friday afternoon when it is traditionally very heavy. The cab was soon stopped in traffic. It was obvious that the bid would not be delivered to the law offices on time. The three attorneys bolted from the cab and sprinted along the sidewalks in a desperate effort to reach Skadden Arps before 5:00.

> When (the) breathless group reached Skadden Arps, their path was blocked by a throng of photographers and television cameras. The newsmen, spotting the portable phone, crowded around and began shouting questions. The attorneys plunged like fullbacks through the assemblage and into the lobby.

* * * * *

> As Truesdell (leader of the group) and his three companions spilled from the elevator on the upper floor, their way was blocked by an enormous security guard. A minute later, Truesdell was escorted into the reception area where, exhausted, he handed over a binder containing the group's bid.
>
> (He) looked at his watch. It was 5:01. The largest takeover bid in corporate history was late. He prayed no one would notice.[2]

On November 29, 1988, the board of directors of RJR Nabisco announced that it would recommend to the stockholders of the company that they accept the new bid from Kohlberg Kravis Roberts at $109 per share. The bid from Ross Johnson and Shearson Lehman Brothers (the one that had arrived at 5:01 on November

23) at $114 was rejected. Complex tax reasons were given for the rejection of the higher offer, but it was widely believed that the original bid at $75 per share, which was now considered to have been far too low, and the compensation package, which had always been considered to have been far too excessive, were also at least partially responsible. Ross Johnson retired from the company he had tried to purchase with a "golden parachute" said to be worth $56 million.

Mr. Johnson obviously benefited from the leveraged buyout of RJR Nabisco, even though he had lost in the bidding process. Who else benefited, who was harmed, and what was the extent of those benefits and harms? The balance of the case will discuss these questions.

It is difficult to tell exactly the extent of benefits and harms in most leveraged buyouts because the published information is so limited. Once a company has been "taken private," the owners no longer have a requirement to file quarterly financial reports. And the reports they do file are not truly comparable to those filed by the earlier firm because so many of the divisions have been sold. It is possible, however, to make some estimates of benefits and harms based upon rules of thumb that are generally accepted in the financial community. Using those rules of thumb, it can be said that the following groups probably will receive reasonably substantial benefits from the leveraged buyout of RJR Nabisco:

1. Members of investor groups can receive huge returns. The actual rate of return depends upon the ability of the investor group to quickly sell some of the divisions, cut many of the expenses, and repay much of the debt before they take the company public once again. The usual rule for a successful buyout is a compound return of 35 percent to 50 percent per year for the five years needed to prepare the company for the public sale. For RJR Nabisco, this would mean a profit of $11.2 billion to $18.9 billion, given an original investment by Kohlberg Kravis Roberts and others of $2.5 billion (10 percent of the total price).

2. Company stockholders also do very well. RJR Nabisco stockholders, including the arbitrageurs who purchased shares only after the first hint of the takeover attempt, were paid $109 per share for stock that had been selling on the open market at $56 per share just five weeks previously. It is said that more than

500 residents of Durham, North Carolina, where the original R. J. Reynolds Tobacco Company had been headquartered and run in paternalistic fashion until the merger with Nabisco, became instant millionaires as a result of stock they had received years earlier as employee benefits. Company stockholders in total received $12.15 billion above the prior market value of the stock as a result of the leveraged buyback.

3. The investment banks receive fees for providing takeover advice and commissions for arranging the sale of corporate junk bonds. The usual rule is that 1.5 percent of the final price goes to the investment banks that are on the winning side. Kohlberg Kravis Roberts had retained Wasserstein Perella, Morgan Stanley, and Drexel Burnham Lambert to assist in the takeover. It is estimated that they received $375 million. The investment banks on the losing side receive far less; it is thought that Shearson and Salomon Brothers shared about $25 million.

4. Merger and acquisition attorneys receive fees both to assist and to fight takeovers. The usual rule is 1 percent of the final price. It is estimated that all of the law firms involved in the RJR leveraged buyout (including Davis Polk, whose attorneys sprinted along the sidewalks of Third Avenue to reach the filing location on time) received $250 million.

5. Commercial banks receive fees to commit the funds needed for the secured loans in the buyout. The usual rule is 0.7 percent of the final price, even though the commercial banks finance only 30 percent to 40 percent of the total, and the rest is raised through the sale of junk bonds. The purchasers of the junk bonds can be further compensated by receiving portions of the equity as sweeteners. These sweeteners cannot be paid to commercial banks (which are forbidden to own the equity of corporate clients) and consequently they receive "commitment fees." The commitment fees from RJR Nabisco were estimated at $175 million.

Who loses when a company is taken private through either a leveraged buyout (outside raiders) or a leveraged buyback (inside management)? The accounting is even more difficult here, for it is difficult to express many of the harms or losses in dollar equivalents, but it is generally believed that three major groups share in the downside:

1. The U.S. government loses due to lower tax receipts. The capital gains of the stockholders are of course taxed when their shares are repurchased at the bid price. The interest payments of the company on the bonds and loans used to finance those repurchases, however, are all tax exempt. The interest payments normally are much larger than the capital gains; consequently, tax revenues to the government decline overall. It has been estimated that the federal government will receive $2.5 billion in capital gains taxes from the takeover of RJR Nabisco but lose $7.5 billion through interest exemptions in the five years following that takeover, for a net loss of $5 billion.

2. The existing bondholders of the company lose due to lower bond ratings. The ratings of the existing corporate bonds are downgraded following issuance of the high-risk junk debt needed to finance the buyback. The new debt does not take precedence over the existing bonds, but the very large increase in the total amount of debt decreases the creditworthiness of the firm and consequently the credit rating of the existing debt. At RJR Nabisco, the long-term debt on the balance sheet increased from $3.88 billion before the buyout to $19.7 million afterward, and the market value of the earlier debt was reduced by more than 30 percent. The State Employees Pension Fund of North Carolina, which had been a substantial investor in the bonds of the R. J. Reynolds Tobacco Company before it merged with the National Biscuit Company, lost $620 million. The close similarity of the loss to the pension fund ($620 million) and the gain to the investment banks ($400 million in total) and law firms ($250 million) did not go unnoticed. The state treasurer said in obvious exasperation, "We could have saved everyone a lot of trouble if they had just sent the bills for the bankers and lawyers directly to us, and forgotten about the buyout."

3. The current employees of the company lose due to company restructuring. It is hard to compare employment numbers and wage/salary payments before and after a leveraged buyout or buyback because so many of the divisions are sold and consequently are no longer included in the data base. It has always been assumed that most of the employees stay with those divisions under the new ownership, but recent evidence seems to indicate that this assumption about continued employment within the disposed divisions may not be warranted as duplicate offices and plants are consolidated and redundant positions are eliminated. It is usually estimated that 20 percent of the employees in the retained divisions are discharged or asked to take early retirement as a result of the cost-saving moves. RJR Nabisco had 120,334 full-time employees prior to the leveraged buyout; if the 20 percent figure is applied to the retained and disposed divisions equally, the number of people adversely affected by the leveraged buyout would be 24,100.

Class Assignment. It has been claimed that leveraged buyouts and buybacks create value for the shareholders and for society. In the instance just described of the leveraged buyout of RJR Nabisco by Kohlberg Kravis Roberts, that claim would appear to be true. The benefits of the transaction have been estimated to total $24,175 million, the harms only $5,620 million, as the following table shows (figures are in millions of dollars):

Investor group benefits, over time	$11,200
Company stockholders, immediate payment	12,150
Investment banks, fees for services	400
Attorneys, fees for services	250
Commercial banks, fees for services	175
Total benefits	$24,175
Government tax losses, net	5,000
Existing bond holder losses	620
Total losses	$ 5,620

Class Assignment. In your opinion, was this leveraged buyout of a major U.S. corporation right or was it wrong? Be prepared to support your belief; don't just say yes or no in class. Why was it right, or why was it wrong?

1. What was the responsibility of Ross Johnson, the chairman and chief executive officer of RJR Nabisco? Assume that he was invited to talk to the class; what would he say? What questions would you ask him? Try to think of questions that he could not answer with a simple yes or no.

2. What were the responsibilities of the investment bankers involved in the leveraged buyout? Why did they act in such an

apparently unprofessional manner when the final bid was being discussed? If Peter Cohen, the managing partner of Shearson Lehman Brothers, came and talked to the class, what questions would you ask him?

3. What were the responsibilities of the attorneys involved in the leveraged buyout? Put yourself in the position of the 26-year-old attorney, Richard Truesdell, who was one of those who sprinted along Third Avenue to reach the law offices of Skadden Arps on time. How would you respond to that question?

4. What are the responsibilities of Louis Gerstner, the person who was put in charge of RJR Nabisco after the leveraged buyout of that company by Kohlberg Kravis Roberts? If he came and talked to the class, what would he say? What questions would you ask him?

Notes

1. *The Wall Street Journal*, January 4, 1990, p. B1.

2. B. Burrough and J. Helyar, *Barbarians at the Gate: The Fall of RJR Nabisco* (New York: Harper & Row, 1990), p. 401.

CHAPTER 3

Managerial Ethics and
the Rule of Law

In this chapter, we will look at the law as a possible basis for managerial decision when one is confronted with an ethical dilemma. The law is a set of rules, established by society, to govern behavior within that society. Why not, then, fall back upon those rules when faced with a conflict between the economic performance of an organization and the social performance of that organization? Why not let the law decide, particularly in a democratic society where the argument can easily be made that the rules within the law represent the collective moral judgments made by members of the society? Why not follow these collective moral judgments, instead of trying to establish our individual moral opinions?

There are numerous examples of laws that do reflect collective moral judgments. Almost everybody within the United States would agree that unprovoked assault is wrong; we have laws against assault. Almost everybody would agree that toxic chemical discharges are wrong; we have laws against pollution. Almost all of us would agree that charitable giving is right; we have no laws against charitable giving. Instead we have laws—provisions within the tax code—that encourage gifts of money, food, and clothing to the poor, and to organizations that work to assist the poor. The question of this chapter is whether we can use this set of rules— often complex, occasionally obsolete, and continually changing—

to form "just" and "proper" and "right" decisions when faced with a choice between our economic gain and our social obligations.

Let me give an illustration of the use of law to justify a decision in an ethical dilemma. The example is a situation that bankers face nearly every day: that between investing in a new, small company that will provide the local community with more job opportunities and higher tax payments to support schools and other needed social services, or loaning the same funds to an established, larger company operating in a distant city. The risk is obviously greater for the first investment, but banks are forbidden by law from charging usurious (too high, or excessive) interest rates to compensate for the risk.

How would you decide in that instance? It is possible, of course, to fall back upon the market and say that the law prohibiting usurious interest rates should be repealed, so that all companies would pay the true costs of their borrowings. Capital is one of the factors of production, along with labor and materials, and the microeconomic argument is that companies should pay prices determined by the factor markets. In this instance, the argument would be that the small, local company should pay the interest rate demanded by a free, efficient, and effective market for loans; if the small local company were unable to pay this risk-adjusted rate, then the money should be invested elsewhere, at the next highest risk-adjusted rate that could be paid, in order to maximize the production of needed goods and services at minimal costs in the use of resources. As was seen in Chapter 2, there are both practical and theoretical problems with this view. The three practical problems are rather basic:

1. Few factor markets, except those for widely available commodities, are truly free in that most tend to be dominated by large corporations and wealthy individuals who determine rather than respond to prices.

2. Few factor markets, again except those for the commodities, are truly efficient in that the full range of price-risk and cost-volume alternatives is not generally known by all participants.

3. Few factor markets—and this is particularly true of the market for capital—are completely effective, because it is difficult to compute the precise risks and accurate costs for different companies in different industries at different times.

The microeconomic response to these three pragmatic problems is that society should add a political process to regulate some prices and allocate some resources, outside of the market process. This proposal, as was also seen in the last chapter, immediately encounters the objection that it requires people to be generously attentive to other people in all political decisions and selfishly attentive only to themselves in all economic activities, and never confuse the two roles. This, it was concluded, is an exceedingly complex and unlikely view of the nature of human beings.

LAW AS A GUIDE TO MORAL CHOICE

We cannot rely upon the market as a guide for managerial decisions and actions when faced with an ethical dilemma, but how about the law? The legal argument is very different. The legal argument is that society has established a set of rules, and that these rules reflect the collective choices of members of society regarding any decisions and actions that affect the welfare of society. This argument can be applied to the particular instance of a bank officer forced to make up his or her mind between a high-risk loan to a small, local company with the return—interest rate—limited by law, and an equivalent loan to a large, distant corporation at much lower risk but equal return—doubtless a higher return if the lower administrative costs of loaning to large, well-financed corporations are included in the calculation. It can be said in this case that society has determined that excessive interest charges are more harmful than limited local support, and that consequently the loan should be given to the larger, distant firm.

Should we object to this decision? Suppose we believe that it is necessary, for the good of our society, that the formation of small, entrepreneurial companies be encouraged. It is often said that if we don't like a given action by a corporation, we should attempt to pass a law either prohibiting that action or encouraging an alternative action, and if we cannot get that law approved through our democratic processes, then we should accept the situation as it exists. That is, we should rely upon the law in our decisions, and agree that if a given act is legal it is "right" and if it is illegal it is "wrong," with the understanding that these determinations of right and wrong can be changed to reflect the majority views of the population. In the example just given, of a bank refusing to advance funds to a high-risk company in the local community and instead providing capital to a lower-risk corporation in a distant city, it would be fairly easy to design corrective legislation. Each bank within the state, or within the nation, could be required to invest a certain percentage of its funds within the communities from which it drew those funds from depositors. This is an aside, of course, but that was essentially the result of the prior laws in most states that prohibited branch banking; local banks were forced to invest within their communities because they had few customer contacts outside of those communities. Deregulation of banks, which ended such territorial restrictions, has also stopped the local service orientation of many financial institutions.

It would also be fairly easy to design a law that would encourage investments in higher-risk, smaller companies. It would be possible, for example, to reduce the risk by providing a governmental guarantee for a given percentage of the loan. This, in effect, was the result of the loan guarantee program of the Small Business Administration—a division of the federal government in the Department of Commerce. Through this program, the government would repurchase 90 percent of the unpaid balance of approved loans in the event of borrower default. Another approach would be to provide a subsidy to the bank or other financial institution to supplement the limited interest rates that may be charged to high-risk companies. That was the effect of the Area Development and Business Investment programs, also from the Small Business Administration, that provided funds at below-market rates to financial institutions for reinvestment in smaller, local firms.

AN EXAMPLE OF MORAL CHOICE

Now, let us return to the banker in the example that was used in the introduction to this chapter. He or she is faced with the decision whether or not to invest in a high-risk local company that will provide employment opportunities and other benefits within the community. Let us agree that this is an ethical dilemma, though in a somewhat mild form, for the choice is between the economic performance of the bank, as measured by potential profits, and the social performance of the same bank, stated in terms of obligations to members of the community. I have suggested that this is a somewhat "mild" ethical dilemma, for no one is going to be hurt very badly by the banker's decision. There will be some employment opportunities lost, and some tax payments not made, but no one will suffer physical harm, as in the unsafe discharge of toxic wastes, or endure emotional stress, as from unfair firing brought about by age, sex, or race discrimination. So, let us strengthen the dilemma. Let us assume that the local community is in an area of high unemployment, that new jobs are badly needed, and that the proposed company is in a labor-intensive, high-growth industry and might eventually create many new jobs. Let us assume that the alternative investment, the large corporation in a distant city, is in a capital-intensive industry and that it would create few new jobs. Let us go even further and assume that the product of the proposed local company is a needed health-care item that would reduce the pain and suffering of elderly patients in hospitals throughout the country, while the product of the alternative investment possibility is a line of high-calorie packaged "junk" foods with low nutritional value. Last, let us not assume but accept the fact that the funds available through the Small Business Administration have been sharply curtailed in recent years and that no governmental guarantee or interest subsidy is available to support the loan to the smaller company. Now we have the classic ethical dilemma: the choice between economic performance and social performance, complicated by extended consequences, uncertain outcomes, and career implications.

How would you decide if faced with this choice? If the banker replies to the founders of the new small company that he or she would very much like to help but that the law prevents an adequate return to compensate for the risk, that no federal guarantees or interest subsidies are available, and that bank officers are required by the legal system to minimize risks for their depositors, can the banker truly be said to be wrong? Of course, the usual response of most bankers to socially desirable but financially shaky loans is not to explain the reasoning that led to the loan rejection. Instead, they merely suggest that the potential borrowers should seek funds elsewhere—where they doubtless will receive exactly the same response.

The question of this chapter is not whether banks should make socially desirable but economically unfeasible loans. Obviously, if the loan cannot be repaid, no bank can make a series of those loans and remain in business. But that is not the issue here. The question is how to make the decision—what factors to consider and what standards to use—in attempting to arrive at a balance between economic performance and social performance. There does have to be a balance. A bank can't make a series of economically feasible but socially undesirable loans either and expect to have the society continue to exist in a form that will enable the bank to prosper. There has to be a limit on both sides. There has to be a balance, and the question is how to achieve that balance.

LAW AS COMBINED MORAL JUDGMENTS

In the last chapter, we looked at the argument that you could achieve the balance between economic and social performance by considering only financial factors and using only economic standards. According to this argument market forces lead inevitably towards maximum social benefits at minimum social costs (Pareto Optimality), and those benefits can then be distributed equitably by a political process. We found that argument wanting. In this chapter we will look at the argument that you should consider both financial and social factors but use legal standards—the requirements of the law—in making ethical or "balanced" choices.

Numerous attorneys and business executives believe that you can base ethical decisions and actions on the requirements of the law. These people would say that if a law is wrong, it should be changed, but that until it is changed it provides a meaningful guide for action. It provides this guide for action, they would add, because each law within a democratic society represents a combined moral judgment by members of our society on a given issue or problem. They will concede that you and I might not agree personally with that judgment on a particular issue, but they would claim that if managers follow the law on that issue, those managers cannot truly be said to be wrong in any ethical sense, since they are following the moral standards of a majority of their peers.

Advocates of the rule of law—a phrase that means the primacy of legal standards in any given social or economic choice—will normally admit that the combined moral judgments represented by the law form a minimal set of standards: the basic rules for living together within a society without infringing on the rights of others. "If you want to go beyond the basic rules of the law in your own decisions and actions," they might say, "we certainly have no objection." "But," they would add, "you cannot require us to go beyond the law, for then you are forcing us to adhere to your moral standards, not those of a majority of the population. We live in a democracy, so, if you don't like something that we are doing, gather together a majority of the voters and pass a law restricting those actions, and we will obey that law. Until then, however, our moral standards are fully as valid as your own, and ours have the support of the majority of the population, so please do not lecture us on your views of what is right or wrong, proper and improper, fair and unfair."

How do we respond to these statements? And if it is not possible to respond logically and convincingly, are we forced to accept the rule of law as determinant in most moral dilemmas? I think that it is necessary first to define the law, so that all of us will recognize that we are discussing the same set of concepts, and then to examine the process—or processes—involved in formulating the law. This examination will be generally the same as in Chapter 2, Managerial Ethics and Microeconomic Theory, in which we looked at the role of market forces as determinants for managerial decisions in ethical dilemmas. However, legal/social/political theory is much less complete than microeconomic theory and there are numerous alternative hypotheses that will have to be considered briefly. First, however, let us define the law and expand on what is meant by the *rule of law*.

DEFINITION OF THE LAW

The law can be defined as a consistent set of universal rules that are widely published, generally accepted, and usually enforced. These rules describe the ways in which people are required to act in their relationships with others within a society. They are requirements to act in a given way, not just expectations or suggestions or petitions to act in that way. There is an aura of insistency about the law; it defines what you *must* do.

These requirements to act, or more generally requirements not to act in a given way—most laws are negative commandments, telling us what we should not do in given situations—have a set of characteristics that were mentioned briefly above. The law was defined as a consistent, universal, published, accepted, and enforced set of rules. Let us look at each of these characteristics in greater detail.

Consistent

The requirements to act or not to act have to be consistent to be considered part of the law. That is, if two requirements contradict each other, both cannot be termed a law, because obviously people cannot obey both.

Universal

The requirements to act or not to act also have to be universal, or applicable to everyone with similar characteristics facing the same set of circumstances, to be considered part of the law. People tend not to obey rules that they believe are applied only to themselves and not to others.

Published

The requirements to act or not to act have to be published, in written form, so that they are accessible to everyone within the society, to be considered part of the law. Everyone may not have the time to read or be able to understand the rules, which tend to be more complex due to the need to precisely define what constitutes similar characteristics and the same set of circumstances. However, trained professionals—attorneys—are available to interpret and explain the law, so that ignorance of the published rules is not considered to be a valid excuse.

Accepted

The requirements to act or not to act in a given way have to be generally obeyed. If most members of the society do not voluntarily obey the law, too great a burden will be placed on the last provision, that of enforcement.

Enforced

The requirements to act or not to act in a given way have to be enforced. Members of society have to understand that they will be compelled to obey the law if they do not choose to do so voluntarily. People have to recognize that if they disobey the law, and if that disobedience is noted and can be proven, they will suffer some loss of convenience, time, money, freedom, or life. There is an aura of insistency about the law; there is also, or should be, an aura of inevitability; it defines what will happen if you don't follow the rules.

This set of rules that are consistent, universal, published, accepted, and enforced—which we call *law*—is supported by a framework of highly specialized social institutions. There are legislatures and councils to form the law; attorneys and paralegal personnel to explain the law; courts and agencies to interpret the law; sheriffs and police to enforce the law. These social institutions often change people's perception of the law because the institutions are obviously not perfect. The adversary relationships of the trial court often seem to ignore the provisions of consistency and universality and to focus on winning rather than justice. The enforcement actions of the police also often seem to be arbitrary and to concentrate on keeping the peace rather than maintaining equity. Let us admit that enforcing the law is a difficult and occasionally dangerous task. Let us also admit that interpreting the law, in court cases, often involves the award of large amounts of money, and that the potential gain or loss of these funds—with attorneys on each side being paid a substantial percentage of that loss or gain—has distorted the concept of the law as a set of published and accepted regulations. But we are looking at the law as an ideal concept of consistent and universal rules to guide managerial decisions, not as a flawed reality.

RELATIONSHIPS BETWEEN THE LAW AND MORAL STANDARDS

If the law is viewed in ideal terms as a set of universal and consistent rules to govern human conduct within society, the question is whether we can accept these rules—flawed though they may be by pragmatic problems in interpretation and enforcement—as representing the collective moral judgment of members of our society. If we can, then we have the standards to guide managerial decisions and actions even though these standards may be at a minimal level. If we cannot accept the set of rules as representing the collective moral judgment of our society, then we will have to look elsewhere for our standards. In considering the possible relationship between moral judgments and legal requirements, there would seem to be three conclusions that can be reached fairly quickly:

　1. The requirements of the law overlap to a considerable extent but do not duplicate the probable moral standards of society. Clearly, a person who violates the federal law against bank robbery also violates the moral standard against theft. And it is easy to show that the laws governing sexual conduct, narcotics usage, product liability, and contract adherence are similar to the moral beliefs that probably are held by a majority of people in our society. I think that we can agree that in a democratic society, the legal requirements do reflect many of the basic values of the citizens, and that there is an area of overlap between the law and morality (see Exhibit 3–1).

　But the area of overlap is not complete. There are some laws that are morally inert, with no ethical content whatever. The requirement that we drive on the right-hand side of the road, for example, is neither inherently right nor inherently wrong; it is just essential that we all agree on which side we are going to drive. There are also some laws that are morally repugnant. Until the early 1960s, some areas of the United States legally required racial

EXHIBIT 3–1
Overlap between Moral Standards and Legal Requirements

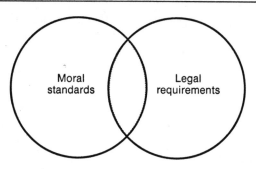

discrimination (segregated education, housing, and travel accommodations), and slavery was legally condoned just 100 years earlier. Finally, there are some moral standards that have no legal standing whatever. We all object to lying, but truthfulness is not required by law except in a court, under oath, and in a few other specific instances such as employment contracts and property sales.

People who believe in the rule of law and accept legal regulations as the best means of governing human conduct within society would respond by saying that it is not at all clear that racial segregation was deplored by a majority of the population prior to 1962, or even that slavery was considered unconscionable before 1862. In a much lighter vein, concerning lying, they might even claim that most people have become accustomed to, and perhaps are amused by, a reasonable lack of truthfulness in advertising messages and political discourse. Moral standards, they would say, are difficult to determine, and we must be careful not to infer that our standards represent those held by a majority of the population.

2. The requirements of the law tend to be negative, while the standards of morality more often are positive. In the law, we are forbidden to assault, rob, or defame each other, but we are not required to help people, even in extreme situations. There is no law, for example, that we must go to the aid of a drowning child. Here, we do have a situation where the moral standards of the majority can be inferred, for doubtless 99.9 percent of the adult population within the United States would go to the aid of a drowning child, to the limit of their ability. People who support the rule of law, however, would say that this instance does not indicate a lack of relationship between moral standards and legal requirements; it only indicates the difficulty of translating one into the other when a positive—compassionate or charitable—act is needed. How, they would question, can you define in consistent and universal terms what is meant by assistance, the characteristics of the person who is to provide that assistance, and the circumstances under which it will be required? This, they would conclude, is just another illustration that the law represents the minimum set of standards to govern behavior in society and that actions beyond that minimum have to come from individual initiative, not legal force.

3. The requirements of the law tend to lag behind the apparent moral standards of society. Slavery, of course, is the most odious example, but sexual and racial discrimination, environmental pollution, and foreign bribery can all be cited as moral problems that were belatedly remedied by legislation. Advocates of the rule of law would say, however, that the evidence of a delay between apparent moral consensus and enacted legal sanctions does not necessarily indicate a lack of relationship between legal requirements and moral standards. It only serves to confirm that relationship, they would claim, for laws controlling discrimination, pollution, and bribery were eventually passed.

None of these arguments—that legal requirements overlap but do not duplicate moral standards, or that the legal requirements appear in different forms (negative rather than positive) and at different times (sequential rather than concurrent)—seems truly decisive. None really helps to determine whether the law really does represent a collective moral judgment by members of a democratic society and consequently can serve to guide managerial decisions and actions. We can easily say that the law does not represent our moral judgment in a given situation, but how can we say that the law in that instance does not represent the moral judgment of a majority of our peers? For that, I think, we have to follow through the process by which our society has developed the law as a universal and consistent set of rules to govern human conduct.

FORMATION OF THE LAW: INDIVIDUAL PROCESSES

Law is obviously a dynamic entity, for the rules change over time. Think of the changes that have occurred in the laws governing employment, for example, or pollution. This is essentially the same point that was made previously, that there seems to be a time lag between changes in moral standards and changes in legal requirements, but actions that were considered to be legal 20 years ago—such as racial and sexual discrimination in hiring, or the discharge of chemical wastes into lakes and streams—are now clearly illegal. The question is whether these changes in the law came from changes in the moral standards of a majority of our population through a social and political process, and consequently whether the law does represent the collective moral standards of our society. The social and political process by which the changing moral standards of individual human beings are alleged to become institutionalized into the formal legal framework of society is lengthy and complex, but a simplified version can be shown in graphic form (see Exhibit 3–2).

Each individual within society has a set of norms, beliefs, and values that together form his or her moral standards. Norms, of course, are criteria of behavior. They are the ways an individual expects all people to act, when faced with a given situation. Foreign students from certain Asiatic countries, for example, bow slightly when addressing a university professor; the bow is their norm or expectation of behavior given that situation. University faculty members within the United States are generally somewhat annoyed when this occurs; their norm or expectation of behavior in that situation is considerably less formal and more egalitarian. The depth of the bow and the degree of annoyance both decline over time as the expectations of behavior on both sides are modified through learning.

Another example of a norm of behavior is considerably less facetious and more relevant to the discussion of moral standards and the law. Most people expect that others, when they meet them, should not cause them injury. Norms are expectations of the ways people ideally should act, not anticipations of the ways people really will act. A person who holds a norm against assault and robbery—as most of us do—will not ordinarily walk down a dark street in the warehouse district of a city at three in the morning; he or she feels that people should not assault and rob each other, not that they will not do so.

Norms are expectations of proper behavior, not requirements for that behavior. This is the major difference between a norm and a law; the norm is not published, may not be obeyed, and cannot be enforced—except by the sanctions of a small group whose members hold similar norms and use such penalties as disapproval or exclusion. Norms also are often neither consistent nor universal. The person who actually commits a crime in the warehouse district at three in the morning, feeling it permissible to assault and rob someone else given the situation and need, doubtless would feel outraged if assaulted and robbed in the same place and at the same time the next night. Norms are just the way

EXHIBIT 3–2
Process by Which Individual Norms, Beliefs, and Values Are Institutionalized into Law

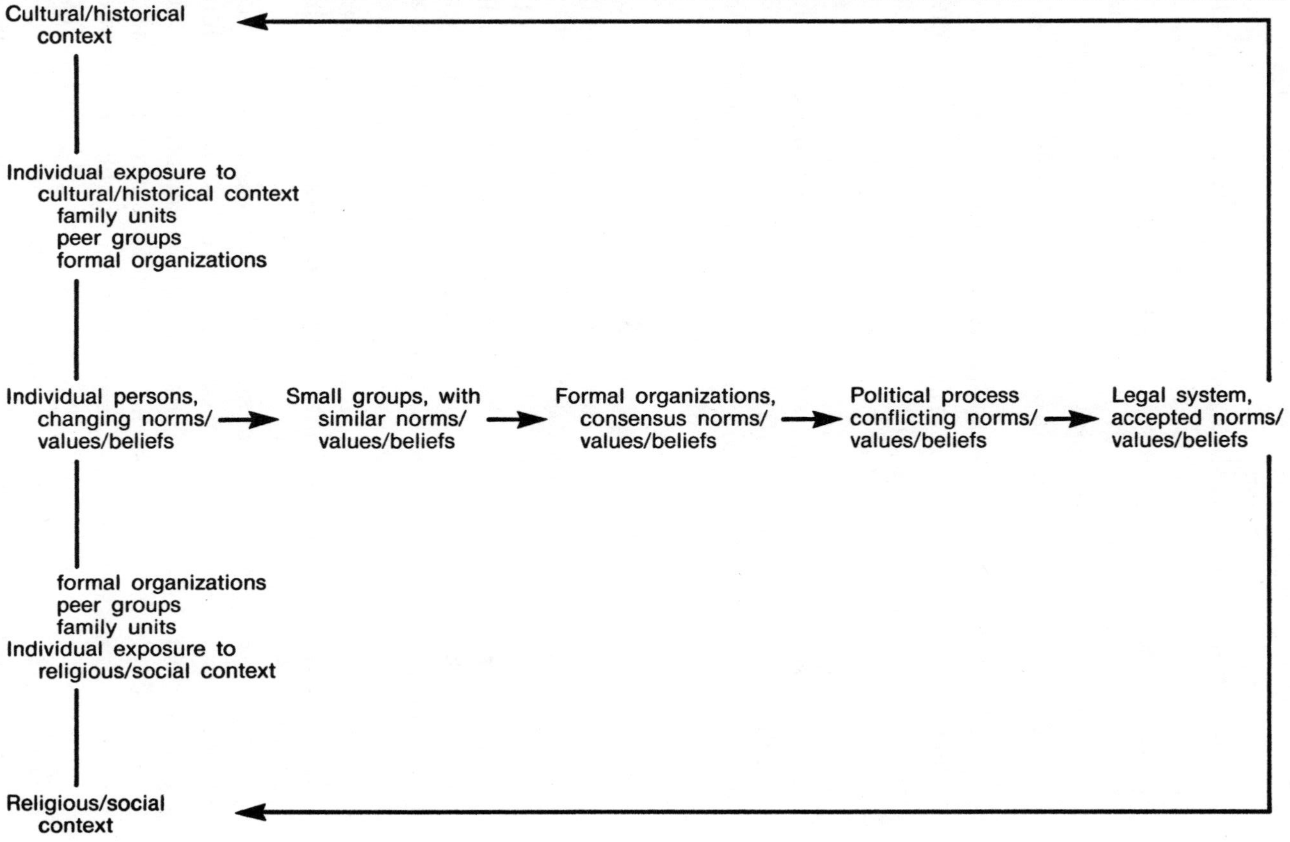

Cultural/historical context →

Individual exposure to cultural/historical context
family units
peer groups
formal organizations →

Individual persons, changing norms/values/beliefs →

Small groups, with similar norms/values/beliefs →

Formal organizations, consensus norms/values/beliefs →

Political process conflicting norms/values/beliefs →

Legal system, accepted norms/values/beliefs

formal organizations
peer groups
family units
Individual exposure to religious/social context →

Religious/social context →

we feel about behavior; often they are neither logically consistent nor universally applied because we have never thought through the reasons we hold them.

Beliefs are criteria of thought; they are the ways an individual expects people to think about given concepts. I believe in participatory democracy, for example, and I expect others to recognize the worth of that concept and accept it as a form of government. I believe in environmental preservation also, and I expect other people to recognize the importance of that idea and accept it as a goal worth working towards.

Beliefs are different from norms in that they involve no action—no overt behavior towards others—just an abstract way of thinking that tends to support an individual's norms. Asiatic students who bow to American professors believe, it is alleged, in a hierarchical society, with definite gradations between older faculty and younger students. People who hold the norm that others should not assault and rob them, even on darkened streets and in deserted neighborhoods, generally believe in the worth of human beings and the preservation of personal property. In one last example, the norm that a company should not bury toxic wastes in leaking 55-gallon drums is associated with beliefs about the benefits of a clean environment and the adverse effects of chemical pollution upon individual health.

Values, the last third of this pattern of personal criteria that together form the moral standards of an individual, are the rankings or priorities that a person establishes for his or her norms and beliefs. Most people do not consider that all their norms and beliefs are equal in importance; generally there are some that seem much more important than others. The important norms and beliefs are the ones that a person "values," or holds in high esteem.

Values often are controversial. Why? Because a norm or belief that one person holds in high esteem can conflict with a different norm or belief that another person holds in equally high esteem. Generally there will be little accommodation or compromise, because each person attaches great importance to his or her criteria of behavior—ways in which people ought to act—and to his or her criteria of belief—ways in which people ought to think. We live in a pluralistic society, with numerous cultural traditions, and in a secular nation, with no accepted or endorsed religious heritage; consequently we have to live with the fact that norms, beliefs, and values will differ among individuals. These differences can and do lead to conflicts.

The norms, beliefs, and values of an individual together form that person's moral standards. Moral standards are our means of judging whether an act that affects others is "right" or "wrong," and they are based upon our personal valuation or ranking of our norms—criteria of behavior—and of our beliefs—criteria of thought. For example, I value highly my norm of nonaggressive behavior between members of our society; if I come out of my house on a summer morning and you hit me on the head and steal my wallet, I am going to consider what you have done to be "wrong." I value less highly my belief in the benefits of a clean environment; if I come out of my house the next day and find you pouring used motor oil down the drain in the street, I am going to think of you as a fairly despicable person, for I would consider that act to be "wrong" also, but less wrong than your previous assault and robbery.

Moral standards—the criteria we use for judging whether an act that impacts others is right or wrong—for now can be considered to be subjective, that is, the result of each individual's emotional preferences among a range of possible norms and beliefs. In the next chapter, Managerial Ethics and Normative Philosophy, we will consider the possibility that moral standards might be seen as objective, or rationally derived from a single fundamental norm or absolute belief. An example of a fundamental norm would be, Always act to generate the greatest good for the greatest number. An example of an absolute belief would be, Justice is the basic essential for a cooperative society. A fundamental norm or absolute belief, if accepted by an individual, would objectively determine that person's complete set of moral standards, because all of his or her other norms and beliefs could be logically derived, in an orderly ranking or value system, from that single principle or truth. A fundamental norm or absolute belief, if accepted by all members of society, would lead to consistent moral standards throughout society, for the same reason. For the present discussion, however, it is necessary to admit that our society lacks such a single principle or truth. This is not to say that we should not have an accepted basis for consistent moral standards; it is just to say that we presently do not have that accepted basis.

FORMATION OF THE LAW: GROUP PROCESSES

Each individual has a set of norms, beliefs, and values that subjectively determine his or her moral standards. These moral standards are at least partially unique to each person, as they are based upon emotional selection rather than rational determination. Most adult members of society recognize their individual set of standards, but few of us have examined or considered these standards beyond a general understanding of mutual reciprocity and social continuance. "I should not assault and rob others because then they would feel free to assualt and rob me" and "I should not assault and rob others because no society can continue to exist if assault and robbery are constant occurrences" are both moral statements, though based upon slightly different sets of norms, beliefs, and values. "I should not assault and rob others because I might get caught and put in jail" is more a legal concern than a moral standard, and it is based upon a very different set of norms, beliefs, and values.

Each individual develops his or her set of norms, beliefs, and values through exposure to the cultural/religious context, the social/political context, and the economic/technological context. Context means the general background or surrounding environment of a situation; the literal derivation of the word is from the Latin "woven together," and that almost exactly conveys the meaning that is intended here. Each society has a background or environment that consists of interwoven threads from religious teachings, cultural traditions, economic conditions, technological developments, social organizations, and political processes. The interwoven nature of the context within which individual choices on norms, beliefs, and values are made ensures that all of these factors interact. Technological changes in communication bring political changes in governance, which cause economic changes in spending and taxation patterns, which eventually result in cultural changes in personal life-style. The exact relationships between economic, technological, social, political, cultural, and religious factors are not known, nor can their combined influences upon an individual's norms, beliefs, and values be predicted with accuracy. But the relationships and influences can easily be observed. Think of the changing status of women, for example, which must have had some origin in the economic shift from heavy manufacturing and mining to knowledge-based and service industries, in the technological development of better birth-control methods, and in the social expansion of educational opportunities. Another illustration of a change in norms, beliefs, and values would be the widespread concern with preservation of the physical environment that developed during the 1960s, and was doubtless influenced by the economic prosperity and political activism of that period.

FORMATION OF THE LAW: SOCIAL PROCESSES

All individuals within a society do not have the same exposures to economic, technological, social, political, cultural, and religious factors. Such exposures come from individual positions, family units, peer groups, and formal organizations. For example, a steel worker who has been unemployed for a number of years due to the closing of a steel mill is directly exposed to the economic reality of international competition; children of the steel worker are indirectly but forcefully exposed through the family unit; associates of the steel worker are indirectly and more lightly exposed through peer groups such as neighborhood associations or social clubs and through formal organizations such as churches and banks. The norms, beliefs, and values of people throughout the industrialized cities that were heavily dependent upon steel, such as Buffalo, Pittsburgh, and Youngstown, have changed over the past 10 years, but to varying degrees, depending upon each individual's exposure to the underlying economic and technological factors.

The changing norms, beliefs, and values of individuals within society do, in a democratic society, have an apparent though delayed impact upon the law. This impact would appear to be the result of both social and political processes. The social process involves, basically, an accretion of power. People with similar norms, beliefs, and values tend to become associated in small groups; it is just natural to join others who have parallel views. These small groups generally are part of much larger organizations, such as business firms, labor unions, political parties, charitable agencies, religious institutions, and veterans' associations, and these larger organizations over time either achieve an acceptable compromise on norms, beliefs, and values, or split into smaller organizations that can achieve such a compromise. There are alternative theories on the means by which this compromise is formed: autocratic decision, bureaucratic adjustment, coalition bargaining, or collective choice. Doubtless all these methods are employed to different degrees in different organizations, but the outcome that can be observed is that many organizations do display a culture of shared norms, beliefs, and values that gradually changes over time.

FORMATION OF THE LAW: POLITICAL PROCESSES

The political process by which the norms, beliefs, and values held by organizations, groups, and individuals are institutionalized into law can be seen basically as a means of resolving conflict. Organizations, groups, and individuals obviously have different opinions on what should be done now (norms) and what should be accomplished in the future (beliefs), and these different views have to be reconciled into consistent and universal rules to be effective. Again, there are alternative theories on the ways by which this is done: presidential leadership, institutional compromise, congressional bargaining, and constituent pressure. The terms would differ at the federal, state, and local levels, but the process doubtless remains approximately the same. The leader, whether president, governor, or mayor, can speak of long-term objectives and attempt to gather support, but he or she has little direct influence on the law-making mechanism. Governmental departments and agencies and nongovernmental lobbying organizations provide the support with information, arguments, and campaign assistance but often must compromise their positions to work jointly and not cancel out each other's influence. Elected representatives are formally assigned responsibility for the formulation of laws in a representative system, but issues differ by section of the country, segment of the population and sector of the economy, and consequently there often seems to be bargaining to establish coalitions to pass most legislation. The public, of course, can express opinions on potential laws by voting for some administrators and all legislators, and indirectly through public surveys, letters, and the media.

The political process by which laws are enacted represents a complex series of interactions. Doubtless no one except a member of Congress or one of the state legislatures fully appreciates the extent and time demands of the formal hearings, office meetings, and committee reports, the constant interruptions and informal exchanges that occur in hallways, parking lots, and evening receptions, and the honest efforts that are made to summarize opinions from the electorate expressed in letters, telephone calls, and the media. All of these help to form the opinions of the legislators. It is easy to be cynical when thinking of the political process, particularly when the high cost of election campaigns is considered and the need to raise money to finance those campaigns is included, but it is difficult to invent a better process than representative democracy.

CONCLUSIONS ON THE RULE OF LAW AS THE BASIS FOR MORAL CHOICE

The question now is whether these social and political processes, lengthy and complex though they may be, truly do serve to combine the personal moral standards of a majority of our population, slowly and gradually, into universal legal requirements. That is, does the law actually represent the collective moral judgment of a majority of our population, or does it just consist of a set of official commands determined by unresponsive legislators? The view that the law does represent collective moral judgment is certainly appealing. However, there would seem to be problems in the transfer from individual moral standards to universal legal requirements at each of the stages in the social and political process.

1. The moral standards of members of society may be based upon a lack of information relative to issues of corporate conduct. Most people were apparently unaware of the payments of large foreign bribes until the revelations of the Lockheed case and the subsequent Securities and Exchange Commission study. Many people now may be unaware of the magnitude of the toxic waste-disposal problem, with 231 million metric tons being produced annually. It is difficult for personal moral standards to influence the law if relevant information is missing.

2. The moral standards of members of society may be diluted in the formation of small groups. People with similar norms, beliefs, and values tend to become associated in small groups, but these standards generally are not precisely similar among all members, and compromises have to be made. Further, many small groups act from motives other than morality; economic benefits and professional prestige often seem to be stressed. It is difficult for personal moral standards to influence the law if they are not conveyed accurately.

3. The moral standards of members of society may be misrepresented in the consensus of large organizations. Many organizations do share norms, beliefs, and values, but there is no evidence that each individual and each group within the organization has equal influence, or even equal weighted influence, in determining that consensus. This can be seen in the norms, beliefs, and values of many nonprofit organizations such as hospitals and universities; the standards of the professional personnel—the physicians and the faculty—often seem to predominate.

4. The moral standards of members of society may be misrepresented in the formulation of the laws. This is the same point that was made above in shaping the consensus of an organization, though on a larger scale. There is no guarantee that all organizations have equal influence, or even equal influence weighted by size, in determining the law. This can be seen in the provisions of much tax legislation; certain organizations always seem to be favored.

5. The legal requirements formed through the political process are often incomplete or imprecise and have to be supplemented by judicial court decisions or administrative agency actions. This can be seen in both product liability cases and equal employment reviews; the meaning and the application of the law have to be clarified outside of the legislative process. It is difficult for personal moral standards to influence the law if they are considered only indirectly—if at all—in two of the means of formulating that law.

What can we say in summary? We can observe that there obviously is an overlap between the moral standards and the legal requirements of our society—the federal law against bank robbery and the moral standard against stealing, for example. And we can see that some changes in the norms, beliefs, and values of individual members of society are eventually reflected by changes in the law—the Foreign Corrupt Practices Act and the Federal Air Pollution Control Act, for example. But we will have to admit that there is no direct relationship in all instances. The social and political processes by which the law is formulated are too complex and too cumbersome—and perhaps too subject to manipulation—for changes in people's norms, beliefs, and values to be directly translated into changes in that set of universal and consistent rules that we call law. Consequently, we cannot view this set of rules as representing the complete collective moral judgment of our society, and therefore we cannot rely totally on the rules when confronted by an ethical dilemma.

The law is a guide to managerial decisions and actions, but it is not enough. And certainly, the absence of a law is not enough to excuse some of those decisions and actions. We need something more. In the next chapter we will look at the fundamental norms and absolute values of normative philosophy as a possible means of providing that "something more."

CASES

When Is It Permissible to Break the Law?

The phrase *to break the law* is overly dramatic. Only two of the situations described below actually involve a person acting in a way that is directly contrary to an existing law. The other three involve situations where the law does not seem to apply, either because the effective date has been delayed, because the practice has not yet been tested in the courts, or because the practice is so recent that it has not yet been considered by the legislature.

1. *Painting billboards in New York City.* It is, of course, illegal to deface private property, and doubtless a claim could be made that it is especially illegal to deface advertising billboards because that act would interfere with the freedom of speech of the advertising firms. Despite that illegality, a group of church members from Harlem in New York City have begun whitewashing billboards advertising cigarettes, liquor, and beer in the inner city. Armed with ladders, long-handled rollers, and buckets of white paint, they have simply painted over advertisements for the offending products. One of the leaders of the group has been quoted as saying, "We have to stop these efforts to market unhealthy products to neighborhoods already overcome by poverty, disease, and despair."[1] In your opinion, is it right to break the law against defacing private property, given that the products being advertised do harm the health of the individuals who buy them?

2. *Reporting improper practices by an auditing client.* Federal law, AICPA (American Institute of Certified Public Accountants) rules, and generally accepted accounting standards all prohibit disclosing confidential information gained during the performance of an audit. In the event that accounting irregularities are discovered, it is expected that the auditing firm will either resign from the assignment or issue an adverse opinion. In the event that nonaccounting irregularities are discovered—such as lax safety practices, self-serving managerial decisions, or illegal political contributions—it has never been determined exactly what actions are required by the auditing firm beyond the overriding prohibition against public disclosure. In your opinion, is it right to break this law against public disclosure of confidential information if an auditing firm does discover evidence of an exceedingly hazardous chemical waste being buried improperly close to a populated area?

3. *Delaying compliance with environmental regulations.* Air conditioning units in automobiles use a coolant containing chlorofluorocarbons (CFCs). Scientists have evidence indicating that CFCs damage the ozone layer of the earth, which provides primary protection against the harmful effects of the sun's radiation. It is feared that skin cancer will increase substantially with the continued deterioration of the ozone layer. (Note: The relationship between CFCs and skin cancer has been proven, unlike the relation between carbon dioxide and global warming, which is still tenuous). In an effort to address this problem, 34 countries ratified a document called the Montreal Protocol, which requires a gradual phase-out of CFC production. The Environmental Protection Agency adopted that phase-out as a federal guideline and called for a 50 percent reduction in CFC usage within the United States by 1998. Non-CFC coolants with potential for use in automotive air conditioners have been developed. Managers at the air conditioner division of one major U.S. automaker recently estimated that they could have a redesigned system ready for implementation by 1993; they requested a $25 million appropriation for the engineering time and testing program. That appropriation request was turned down by the corporate staff, with the statement that it was not cost-effective to make the change (which was estimated to add $40 to $50 to the price of each car) before it was required by law. In your opinion, is it right to delay design changes until absolutely required by the law, given that that delay will cause further harm to the environment?

4. *Rewarding company employees for "whistleblowing" against their employer.* The VSI Corporation of Seattle, Washington, is the world's largest manufacturer of aircraft bolts and fasteners. Aircraft bolts and fasteners must be of exceedingly high quality, lightweight yet strong, and very resistant to rust and metal fatigue. They are made of titanium, aluminum, and special alloys of steel. In May of 1990, the company agreed to pay a federal fine of $18 million on charges that over a period of seven years it had falsified metallurgical tests on the millions of bolts and fasteners it had sold to the civilian and military aircraft industries. The metallurgical tests were destructive in nature—that is, they destroyed the part that was being tested—and consequently they had not been repeated by the company's customers. The prosecuting attorney admitted that no accidents had been traced to the poorly tested fasteners and that most bolts and fasteners now in inventory or in use did meet most of the original specifications.

The disturbing issue, from the viewpoint of some industry participants, was the fact that the two employees of VSI Corporation who had reported the test falsifications to the federal government and had provided secretly videotaped proof of those falsifications were to receive an award of 25 percent of the fine, under the provisions of a 1988 federal law that was designed to encourage whistleblowing. An aircraft industry executive described his concerns verbally as follows: "No one is defending the practice of falsifying quality checks on critical parts, but the federal government is paying two employees $2.25 million each for spying on their employer. With that sort of reward, every employee in the country is going to start looking for wrongdoing, and may encourage or even generate a little wrongdoing just to get the money. $2.25 million is like winning the lottery. The federal government is bribing the employees of private companies." In your opinion, is it right for the federal government to pay company employees very substantial amounts of money to report company wrongdoing, given that in the past (without the payment) many similar wrongdoings did go unreported?

5. *Providing special discounts to large corporations.* It has recently been disclosed that airlines and hotels have been negotiating special rates for the large corporations that are, of course, large users of their services.[2] Special rates on the airlines for these customers were said to be 32 percent below the fares for the advance-purchase coach tickets available to everyone else, though without the restrictions for advance purchases, and weekend stay-overs that applied to others. Special rates at the hotels for these customers were said to average 22 percent less than those assigned to members of the general public.

The reason for these special rates is clear: The airlines and hotels compete for the business of the large corporations, which account for 60 percent of all travel expenditures. Legally, it is permissible for suppliers to offer special rates for goods or services to large corporations if it can be shown that those rates reflect economies of scale in providing the goods and services. Small business management associations and travel agency trade groups have claimed that those economies of scale do not exist in air travel and hotel accommodations because the reservations are made and the services are provided for individuals, not for groups, and consequently the charges should be equal for all. A representative of one of the trade groups explained his views verbally as follows: "A business executive from a large company in Philadelphia and my mother from a small town in Pennsylvania both fly nonstop from Philadelphia to Minneapolis at the same time and on the same plane and then return at the same time and on the same plane. The ticket costs my mother $326 and the executive $204. That is not right. It is not against the law because we have not yet been able to get a hearing before a court, but it is still not right." In your opinion, is it right to offer special discounts to large corporations, given that discounts apparently are made up by higher charges to smaller firms and private individuals?

Class Assignment.   Decide which of these actions are right and which are wrong. Follow your own opinion, but be prepared to support that opinion. Don't just give your answers in class and then stop; instead be ready to say why you think they are right or why you think they are wrong.

Notes

1. *New York Times*, April 10, 1989, p. 3.
2. *New York Times*, January 15, 1990, p. 26, and *The Wall Street Journal*, March 12, 1990, p. B1.

Susan Shapiro

Susan Shapiro has an undergraduate degree in chemistry from Smith College, a master's degree in chemical engineering from M.I.T., three years service as a sergeant in the Israeli army, and an MBA from the University of Michigan. The following is a nearly verbatim account of her experiences during the first month of employment with a large chemical company in New York.

We spent about three weeks in New York City, being told about the structure of the company and the uses of the products, and then they took us down to Baton Rouge to look at a chemical plant. You realize that most of the MBAs who go to work for a chemical company have very little knowledge of chemistry. There were 28 of us who started in the training program that year, and the others generally had undergraduate degrees in engineering or economics. I don't know what you learn by looking at a chemical plant, but they flew us down South, put us up at a Holiday Inn, and took us on a tour of their plant the next day.

As part of the tour, we were taken into a drying shed where an intermediate chemical product was being washed with benzine and then dried. The cake was dumped in a rotating screen and sprayed with benzine, which was then partially recovered by a vacuum box under the screen. However, the vacuum box technology is out-of-date now, and never did work very well. Much of the solvent evaporated within the shed, and the atmosphere was heavy with the fumes despite the open-air type of construction.

Benzine is a known carcinogen; there is a direct, statistically valid correlation between benzine and leukemia and birth defects. The federal standard is 10 parts per million, and a labor director would get upset if you let the concentration get near 100 parts for more than a few minutes, but in the drying shed it was over 1,000. The air was humid with the vapor, and the eyes of the men who were working in the area were watering. I was glad to get out, and we were only in the drying shed about three minutes.

I told the foreman who was showing us around—he was a big, burly man with probably 30 years' experience—that the conditions in the shed were dangerous to the health of the men working there, but he told me, "Lady, don't worry about it. That is a sign-on job [a job to which newly hired employees are assigned until they build up their seniority so that they can transfer to more desirable work]. We've all done it, and it hasn't hurt any of us."

That night back at the motel, I went up to the director of personnel, who was in charge of the training program, and told him about the situation. He was more willing to listen than the foreman, but he said essentially the same thing. "Susan, you can't change the company in the first month. Wait awhile; understand the problems, but don't be a troublemaker right at the start."

The next morning, everybody else flew back to New York City. I stayed in Baton Rouge and went to see the plant manager. I got to his office by 8:00 and explained to his secretary why I wanted to see him. He was already there, at work, and he came out to say that he was "up against it that morning" and had no time to meet with me. I said, "Fine, I'll wait."

I did wait until after lunchtime. Then he came up to me and said he didn't want to keep tripping over me every time he went in and came out of his office, and if I would just go away for a while, he would promise to see me between 4:30 and 5:00.

It was 5:15 when he invited me to "come in and explain what has you so hot and bothered." I told him. He said that he certainly knew what I was talking about and that every year he put a capital request into the budget to fix the problem, but that it always came back rejected—"probably by some MBA staff type" were his words—because the project could not show an adequate return on investment and because the present process was technically open-air and therefore not contrary to Occupational Safety and Health Administration (OSHA) regulations.

I started to explain that OSHA never seemed to know what it was doing—which is true, in my opinion. But he stopped me. He said that he was leaving to pick up his family because his daughter was playing in a Little League baseball game at 6:30, and then they would have supper at McDonald's. He said I could go along if I didn't mind sitting next to his five-year-old son, who held "the world's record for the number of consecutive times he has spilled his milk in a restaurant." He was a very decent man, working for a very indecent company. I told him I would go back to New York and see what I could do. He did wish me good luck, but he also asked me not to get him personally involved because, he said, "Insisting upon funding for a project that won't meet targeted rates of return is a surefire way to be shown the door marked exit in large black letters."

Class Assignment.   What would you do in this situation? Make a set of specific recommendations for Susan Shapiro.

Rights of the Corporate Stakeholders

A business firm can be viewed in a number of different ways. One view is that of traditional economic theory: A corporation is a collection of assets owned by the stockholders and managed to optimize the return upon those assets. Another view is that of the law: A corporation is a legal entity chartered by the government and managed to stay within the terms of that charter. A third view is that of organizational theory: A corporation is an association of individuals, managed to ensure the ongoing productivity of those employees.

All three theories accept the priority of the stockholders. The return on the assets, the terms of the charter, and the productivity of the employees are for the benefit of the owners, that is, the stockholders in the firm.

The "stakeholder" approach to management is different. This theory looks upon a corporation as composed of groups of people both internal (workers, managers, and owners) and external (customers, suppliers, distributors, creditors, etc.) to the firm. The owners do not necessarily take precedence over the others. Instead, each of the groups is said to have certain rights, or "stakes," in the operations of the enterprise. For example, a person who believed in the stakeholder approach would claim that company employees who have worked faithfully and well over a lengthy period of time have certain rights, and it is the responsibility of management to recognize those rights *relative* to the rights of the other groups, such as the owners.

Class Assignment. Begin to think about this stakeholder approach to the ethics of management. Listed below are 10 groups of people both internal and external to the firm. Does the firm have any duties or obligations to the people in those groups? If so, what exactly are those duties and obligations? You can add some additional groups if you want (e.g., competitors), or you can subdivide some of the existing groups (e.g., recently hired, long-service, and currently retired persons among the employees). Last, if you were going to look at a college or university as a collection of groups of people with certain rights or stakes in the operations of the institution, what are those groups and what are those rights?

1. Customers
2. Employees (hourly paid)
3. Managers (salaried)
4. Suppliers
5. Distributors
6. Creditors
7. Owners
8. Local residents
9. National citizens
10. Global inhabitants

CHAPTER 4

Managerial Ethics and Normative Philosophy

The ethical dilemma in management centers on the continual conflict, or on the continual potential for that conflict, that exists between the economic and the social performance of an organization. Business firms have to operate profitably or they will not survive over the long term; that is their economic performance. Business firms also have to recognize their obligations to employees, customers, suppliers, distributors, stockholders, and the general public; that is their social performance. The problem—and the essence of the ethical dilemma in management—is that sometimes improvements in economic performance—increases in sales or decreases in costs—can be made only at the expense of one or more of the groups to whom the organization has some form of obligation. The economies of scale that follow a merger can be achieved only if the surplus employees are discharged or demoted. The benefits of direct factory-to-store distribution can be realized only if the existing wholesalers are replaced. The advantages of hydroelectric power can be realized only if a river valley is flooded and local residents are forced to move.

How do we decide when faced with these issues? How do we find the balance between economic performance and social performance that is "right" and "proper" and "just"? There are only three forms of analysis—ways of thinking about the dilemma and arriving at the balance that can be used:

Economic Analysis, Based on Impersonal Market Forces. The belief is that a manager should always act to maximize revenues and minimize costs, for this strategy, over the long term, will produce the greatest material benefits for society, and those benefits can be equitably distributed by political, not economic, means. As we saw, there are both practical and theoretical problems with that approach, so we cannot rely on economic analysis to resolve ethical conflicts; it certainly helps to know the financial revenues and costs, but something more is needed.

Legal Analysis, Based on Impersonal Social and Political Processes. The belief is that a manager should always act to obey the law, for the law within a democracy represents the collective moral judgment of members of society. Again, there are both practical and theoretical problems with that view, so we cannot rely on legal analysis, either by itself or in conjunction with economic analysis, to resolve ethical conflicts. It certainly helps to know the legality of a situation, but something even further is needed.

Philosophic Analysis, Based on Rational Thought Processes. The view is that a manager should always act in accordance with either a single principle of behavior or a single statement of belief that is "right" and "proper" and "just" in and by itself. This is "moral reasoning"; logically working from a first principle through to a decision on the duties we owe to others. There are some problems here also, though perhaps not as serious as in the other two instances.

Moral reasoning requires an understanding of normative philosophy. It is not possible to summarize normative philosophy in a single chapter—just as, quite frankly, it is not really possible to summarize microeconomic relationships or social/political processes in a single chapter—but it is possible to convey some of the basic concepts and methods, provided the reader is interested and willing to think about them. I assume that you are interested or you would not have gotten this far.

DEFINITION OF NORMATIVE PHILOSOPHY

Philosophy is the study of thought and conduct. Normative philosophy is the study of the proper thought and conduct; that is,

how we should behave. Normative philosophers have been looking at these issues for more than 2,400 years—since the time of
Plato, who lived from 427 to 347 B.C. They have attempted to
establish a logical thought process, based upon an incontrovert-
ible first principle, that would determine whether an act was
"right" or "wrong," "good" or "evil," "fair" or "unfair." They have
not been successful—otherwise all that would be needed would be
to quote the sources and state the findings—but many of their
concepts and methods are relevant to managerial ethics. All hard
ethical decisions are compromises, between economic and social
performance in the case of a business firm, between wants and
duties in the case of an individual. Normative philosophy provides some help in making those compromises, but that help is not
as extensive as one might wish. Here, then, is an introduction to
the normative philosophy of morality and ethics.

First, there is a difference between morality and ethics. Morality refers to the standards of behavior by which people are
judged, and particularly to the standards of behavior by which
people are judged in their relationships with others. A person in
the midst of a desert, isolated from anyone else, might act in a way
that was immature, demeaning, or stupid, but he or she could not
truly be said to have acted immorally since that behavior could
have no impact upon others, unless it were to waste water or other
resources needed by travelers in the future. Ethics, on the other
hand, encompasses the system of beliefs that supports a particular
view of morality. If I believe that a person should not smoke in a
crowded room, it is because I have accepted the research findings
of some scientists and the published statements of the Surgeon
General that tobacco smoke is harmful; my acceptance of those
findings is my ethic, for that particular situation. Ethics is normally used in the plural form since most people have a system of
interrelated beliefs rather than a single opinion. The difference
between morality and ethics is easy to remember if one speaks of
moral standards of behavior and ethical systems of belief, and I
will use those terms in this discussion.

ETHICAL RELATIVISM

The next issue to be addressed in this description of the techniques of moral reasoning is that of ethical relativism. The question here is very basic: Are there objective universal principles

upon which one can construct an ethical system of belief that is applicable to all groups in all cultures at all times? Moral standards of behavior differ between groups within a single culture, between cultures, and between times. This is obvious. For example, within the contemporary United States, moral standards for decisions on product safety differ between the leaders of consumer interest groups and the executives of major industrial corporations, and it is probable that these standards of product safety would differ even more greatly between the United States and the Middle East, or between the contemporary period and the late 19th century. The ethical systems of belief supporting those moral standards of behavior also differ; each group, in each country, in each time period, can usually give a very clear explanation of the basis for its actions. To continue the earlier example, representatives of consumer interest groups can provide a perfectly logical reason for their support of a mandatory requirement that air bags be installed in passenger cars, and managerial personnel from the automotive manufacturing companies can offer an equally logical reason for their opposition to such a requirement. Both sides base their arguments on a system of beliefs as to what is best for the national society, but unfortunately those beliefs differ. I think we can all agree that among the most irritating aspects of the debate over ethical issues such as product safety are the attitudes of personal self-righteousness and the implications of opponent self-interest that seem to pervade all these discussions. Both sides assume that their systems of belief are so widely held, and so obviously logical, that their opponents have to be small-minded and illiberal; they do not recognize the legitimate differences that can exist between ethical systems as to what is "right" or "proper" or "good" for the country.

The question in ethical relativism is not whether different moral standards and ethical beliefs exist; they obviously do, and we all have experiences to confirm that fact. The question is whether there is any commonality that overrides the differences. In the mixed chorus of competing moral standards and diverse ethical systems, can we discern any single principle that unifies them all, or are we left with the weak and unsatisfactory conclusion that all ethical systems are equally valid, and that a person's choice has to be relative to his or her upbringing or education or position or country or culture. If all ethical systems are equally valid, then no firm moral judgments can be made about individual behavior, and we are all on our own, to do as we like to others, within economic and legal constraints.

Fortunately, there is one principle that does seem to exist across all groups, cultures, and times and that does form part of every ethical system; that is the belief that members of a group bear some form of responsibility for the well-being of other members of that group. There is a widespread recognition that men and women are social beings, that cooperation is necessary for survival, and that some standards of behavior are needed to ensure that cooperation. In one of the most famous statements in ethical philosophy, Thomas Hobbes (1588–1679) argued that if everyone acted on the basis of his or her own self-interest and ignored the well-being of others, life would be "solitary, nasty, brutish, and short."

People in all cultures, even the most primitive, do not act solely for their own self-interest, and people in those cultures understand that standards of behavior are needed to promote cooperation and ensure survival. These standards of behavior can be either negative—it is considered wrong to harm other members of the group—or positive—it is considered right to help other group members—but they do exist and can be traced in both sociological and anthropological studies. Consequently, the important question in moral relativism is not whether your moral standards are as good as mine; it is whether your moral standards that benefit society are as good as mine that benefit society.[1] The second question is very different from the first; it forces both of us to justify our standards relative to a principle that does extend over groups, cultures, and times. We can say that our definitions of what is "right" differ, and we can each act in accordance with those definitions and believe that we are morally correct; yet the way in which we determine what is "right" is the same.

The fact that there can be two different moral standards, both of which can be considered to be "right," is confusing to many people. Let me try to clarify this apparent paradox with an example, and we will use the familiar example of the Brazilian customs. Let us say that I am from that South American country, and I believe it is morally acceptable to pay small bribes to the customs agents in order to expedite import clearance and shipment. You, on the other hand, are from the United States, and you find the practice to be morally unacceptable. We differ, though I work for you, in the same company, so I don't dwell on the differences. You come to Brazil; together we shepherd an important shipment through customs. You return to New York and tell your friends at lunch, "I had to pay." They are shocked, or would be if South American customs officials were not so notorious. I have dinner with friends that night, and tell them, "The man didn't want to pay." They are shocked, or would be if North American business practices were not often thought to be so bizarre. Both of us are right, as long as we base our standards on what we believe to be best for society. I think, "Customs agents need the money; our government sets their salary assuming that they make a small percentage"; you think, "The system would work better if everyone were much more honest." Both of our standards are based upon what we believe to be best for our society; consequently both are "right." Now, if we had the time and wanted to make the effort, we could search for a universal principle that would help us define what we meant by "best" for our society, and if we could measure that benefit, then we might be able to agree on which of our standards was more "right." What I am trying to explain, using this illustration, is that two different moral standards can both be *believed* "right"; that is not the same thing as saying that the two different moral standards *are* "right." We have to accept the proposition that we bear some responsibility for other members of our society or life becomes very "solitary, nasty, brutish, and short," for us as well as for others. That responsibility becomes the absolute upon which our ethical systems are based.

This is somewhat in the nature of an aside, but the question of moral relativism—whether moral standards are valid across groups and cultures and times, or whether moral standards just depend upon individual and social and cultural circumstances—is sometimes applied to business firms. It is possible to think of business as a "game" in which different rules apply than in everyday life—a game similar to poker or dice in which no one expects the truth to be fully spoken or contracts to be fully honored.[2] Game strategy, it is said, requires exaggerations and concealments in making statements; the hearer has to be vigilant. Game outcome, it is alleged, encourages shortfalls in fulfilling contracts; the buyer has to be wary.

It is not difficult to find evidence of this "game" approach to business. Company-union wage negotiations are seldom examples of verisimilitude. Public accountants would not be needed if all financial figures were accurately reported. There is a reason that gas pumps and grocery scales are inspected by a public agency and sealed to prevent tampering.

What do you think of this view of management as a game, in which almost any act is permitted that the other side does not detect and offset, a game in which the rules are set by the players, using their moral standards, which are "fully as good as anyone else's"? How would you argue against this view? You should come back to the absolute of some responsibility for other members of society, which has been exhibited by every other culture at every other time, and you set the rule that their moral standards *that benefit society* are fully as good as anyone else's that benefit society. The standards of lying and cheating benefit only the liar and the cheater; if those standards are applied to everyone, the advantages disappear, and society becomes impossible, with no truth and no trust.

Given that you accept the basic premise that both you and I bear some form of responsibility for other people within our society, and that our society cannot continue to exist without some standards of behavior between individuals and groups, how do we determine whether those standards are "right" or "wrong"? We all have an intuitive understanding of right and wrong, but we don't know exactly how to classify our own actions, or those of our neighbors.

The universal recognition that we owe something to other people within our society, and that we are bound by a concept of right and wrong in our behavior to those people, has to be made operational. That is, we have to establish some consistent analytical method to classify our actions as "right" or "wrong." If we can't, it's not for lack of trying. As mentioned before, intellectual history over the past 2,400 years has been filled with attempts to justify moral standards and to establish ethical systems. None works perfectly, but there are five major systems that do have a direct relevance to managerial decisions: Eternal Law, Utilitarian Theory, Universalist Theory, Distributive Justice, and Personal Liberty.

ETERNAL LAW

Many church leaders and some philosophers (Thomas Aquinas and Thomas Jefferson among them) believe that there is an Eternal Law, incorporated in the mind of God, apparent in the state of Nature, revealed in the Holy Scripture, and immediately obvious to any man or woman who will take the time to study either nature or the Scripture. Thomas Jefferson, really the first of the secular humanists, believed that the truths of this law were "self-evident," in his famous phrase, that the rights were "inalienable," and that the duties could easily be derived from the rights. If people had rights to "life, liberty and the pursuit of happiness," then they had obligations to ensure those rights to others, even if this meant revolution against the British Crown. Religious leaders tend to emphasize the revealed source of the truth more than the reasoned nature, but they also believe that the state of the Law is unchanging, and that the rights and duties are obvious: if we are Loved, then we must love others.[3] This reciprocal exchange is summarized in Christian theology by the Golden Rule: Do unto others as you would have others do unto you.

What is wrong with Eternal Law or Natural Law, interpreted by either religious leaders or normative philosophers, as the basis for an ethical system in management? Nothing, except for the number of interpretations. No two Natural Law theorists, and very few religious writers, have ever been able to agree on the exact provisions of the revealed or reasoned truth. Each religion provides moral standards for its members, and many of the members observe those standards in daily life, but the standards differ between groups, and there is no way to determine which one is "right" or "best" or "proper" for the full society. Even the Golden Rule, that simple, elegant, sensible guide to life, can't somehow be applied universally. If you were a wealthy person, you would possibly want others to retain their wealth, and you would expect to be treated the same way. If I were a poor person, I would wish others to share their income and benefits, just as I would be willing to share the little I had. Religious rules of conduct tend to be situation dependent; that is, our interpretation of them seems to vary with our personal circumstances. This may happen because most of our religious injunctions for moral behavior were developed many years ago in an agricultural society that had greater equality between individuals but less liberty for each person; the rules are not easily applied in an industrial society with those conditions exactly reversed.

UTILITARIANISM: A TELEOLOGICAL THEORY

The teleological approach to managerial ethics places complete emphasis upon the outcome, not the intent, of individual actions. Teleology is derived from a Greek term that means outcome or result, and some of the most influential philosophers in the Western tradition—including Jeremy Bentham and J. S. Mill—have held that the moral worth of personal conduct can be determined solely by the consequences of that behavior. That is, an act or decision is "right" if it results in benefits for people, and it is "wrong" if it leads to damages or harm; the objective obviously is to create the greatest degree of benefits for the largest number of people while incurring the least amount of damages or harm.

The benefits can vary. Material benefits are not the only ones that count, though they are certainly a good starting place for the calculations, but friendships, knowledge, health, and the other satisfactions we all find in life should be included as well. Think in terms of satisfactions, not pleasures; focusing on pleasures can lead to a very hedonistic and self-centered approach. The aggregate satisfactions or benefits for everyone within society have to be considered.

The benefits are not all positive. There are negative costs and adverse outcomes associated with each action, and they have to be included to establish a balance. The negative costs and adverse outcomes include pain, sickness, death, ignorance, isolation, and unhappiness. The aggregate harms or costs have to be considered, and then a balance of the net consequences can be computed.

This teleological ethical system—focusing on net consequences, not individual intentions—is termed Utilitarianism, a philosophy originated by Jeremy Bentham (1748–1832), a British thinker. The name of the philosophy is derived from the word utility, which had an 18th-century meaning that referred to the degree of usefulness of a household object or a domestic animal; that is, a horse could be said to have a utility for plowing beyond the cost of its upkeep. Utility has this same meaning, and this same derivation, in microeconomic theory; it measures our degree of preference for a given good or service relative to price. In Utilitarian theory, the term refers to our perception of the net benefits and costs associated with a given act.

Utilitarianism is obviously close to the economic concept of cost/benefit analysis, particularly as the benefits are not to be confused with expediency and have to be calculated for the long-term consequences as carefully as for the short-term outcomes. Utilities, both benefits and costs, have to be computed equally for everyone. My satisfactions, and my costs, cannot be considered to be more important in some way than your satisfactions, and your costs. The decision rule that is then followed is to produce the greatest net benefits for society; an act is "right" if, and only if, it produces greater net benefits for society than any other act possible under the circumstances. There are, of course, problems in measuring net benefits—the combination of positive and negative outcomes associated with the act—but mathematical precision is not required; we can approximate the outcomes and include them in our calculations.

Utilitarianism differs from the economic concept of cost/benefit analysis in that the distribution of the costs and benefits has to be included as well. That is, these are net benefits to society, and each individual within the society has to be considered equally, and treated equally in the distribution. "The greatest good for the greatest number" takes precedence in Utilitarian theory over "The greatest good for a smaller, more elite number."

To save time, and to avoid the need to compute the full consequences of every decision and action, most Utilitarians recommend the adoption of simplifying rules. These rules, such as "always tell the truth" or "never renege on a contract" can be logically shown to lead to beneficial outcomes in all foreseeable cases, but the basis for the rules remains the balance of positive and negative consequences that come from every act or decision.

What is wrong with Utilitarianism? Not very much, except for the possibility of exploitation. In the vast majority of cases, where no one is going to be hurt very badly, and particularly where it is possible to use financial equivalents for both the costs and the benefits, it is a familiar and useful form of analysis. But, there is always the possibility of justifying benefits for the great majority of the population by imposing sacrifices or penalties on a small minority. For example, substantial benefits could be brought to large numbers of the American people by expropriating all the property of the readers of the *Harvard Business Review*. This proposal, which might win the approval of a few truly liberal economists and a few extremely opportunistic politicians, would hopefully be rejected by all normative philosophers. Utilitarianism fails because in reality it is two principles: greatest good and greatest number; at some point in our decision processes on important matters, these two principles come into conflict, and then we have no single means of determining what is the "right" or "best" or "proper" act.

Last, Utilitarianism fails because we can probably all agree that there are some actions that are simply wrong, despite great apparent net benefits for a huge majority. Dostoevsky provided the extreme example. In *The Brothers Karamazov* he asked what should be done if the happiness of the whole human race, forever, could be brought about by the sacrifice of only one person, one completely innocent child, who would have to be tortured to death. No one should ever be able to accept that exchange. Teleological theory fails as a determinant of moral actions because it is impossible to balance the benefits of the majority against the sacrifices of a minority.

UNIVERSALISM: A DEONTOLOGICAL THEORY

The deontological approach to managerial ethics, in essence, is the reverse of teleological theory. Deontology is derived from another Greek term referring to the duties or the obligations of an individual. This ethical theory states that the moral worth of an action cannot be dependent upon the outcome because those outcomes are so indefinite and uncertain at the time the decision to act is made; instead, the moral worth of an action has to depend upon the intentions of the person making the decision or performing the act. If I wish the best for others, then my moral actions are praiseworthy, even though I happen to be an ineffectual and clumsy individual who always seems to be breaking something or hurting someone. It is assumed that we are not all clumsy and ineffectual people, and therefore that good intentions will normally result in beneficial outcomes.

Personal intentions can be translated into personal duties or obligations because, if we truly wish the best for others, then we will always act in certain ways to ensure beneficial results, and those ways become duties that are incumbent upon us rather than choices that are open to us. It is our duty to tell the truth; it is our duty to adhere to contracts; it is our duty not to take property that belongs to others. (Truthfulness, legality, and honesty can be logically derived from the basic principles of all ethical systems; in deontological theory they are duties we owe to others, while in teleological theory they are the actions that bring the greatest benefits to others.)

Our personal duties are universal, applicable to everyone, and consequently much of deontological theory is also termed Universalism, just as large portions of teleological theory are called Utilitarianism. The first duty of Universalism is to treat others as ends and not as means. Other people should be seen as valuable ends in themselves, worthy of dignity and respect, and not as impersonal means to achieve our own ends. No action can be considered "right" in accordance with personal duty if it disregards the ultimate moral worth of any other human being.

Immanuel Kant (1724–1804) proposed a simple test for personal duty and goodwill, to eliminate self-interest and self-deception, and to ensure regard for the moral worth of others. The test is to ask yourself whether you would be willing to have everyone in the world, faced with similar circumstances, forced to act in exactly the same way. This is the Categorical Imperative; "categorical," of course, means absolute or unqualified, and the precept is that an act or decision can be judged to be "good" or "right" or "proper" only if everyone must, without qualification, perform the same act or reach the same decision, given similar circumstances.

Kant starts with the simple proposition that it is unfair for me to do something that others don't do or can't do or won't do. This is not because the total effects upon society might be harmful if everyone took the same action such as refusing to pay taxes—that would be a utilitarian doctrine based upon outcomes rather than a universalist precept based upon duties—but because I owe others the duty of acting consistently. I have a "will," or a view of the way I want the world to be, and my views must be consistent or I would have a "contradiction in wills," which is not fair to others given my duty to act rationally and consistently. That is, I pay taxes not because if everyone else did not pay taxes the government would collapse and there would be chaos, but because I want a world of law and order, and therefore I must also want to provide the financial support for that law and order. Law and order and taxes are right for me if, and only if, they are right for everyone else—that is, if they are "universalizable." Kant can be understood as an attempt to tie moral actions to rational decisions, with rationality defined as being based upon consistent and universal maxims. Moral standards, according to Kant, are based upon logical consistency.

The two formulations by Kant—(1) to act only in ways that I would wish all others to act, faced with the same set of circumstances, and (2) always to treat other people with dignity and respect—can be viewed as a single injunction. The first version says that what is morally right for me must be morally right for others. Everyone is of equal value. If this is so, then no person's rights should be subordinated to those of anyone else. If that is so, then we must treat people as free and equal in the pursuit of their interests.

Universalism, particularly when supported by the Categorical Imperative test, is a familiar and useful guide to behavior. The common law is a form of Universalism: Everyone, faced with a just debt, should pay that debt and no one, needing money, should rob banks. Company policies that have a legal or ethical content are usually Universalist: All personnel managers, in considering promotions and pay increases, should include length of service as well as individual ability; and no product manager, in setting prices, should contact competitors or agree to trade constraints.

What is wrong with Universalism? It is a useful method of moral reasoning, but there are no priorities and there are no degrees. I might will law and order to be absolute, with no opposition to the government outside of the formal electoral process, while you might prefer greater personal freedom. I might will that everyone pay taxes at 7 percent of their annual income, while you might believe that a graduated income tax would be more equitable. Universalism is another ethical system that seems to be very dependent for interpretation upon the situation of the individual. Even the more basic formulation of the Categorical Imperative—to treat each other as moral objects, worthy of respect and dignity—provides very limited help. It is difficult to treat others as ends and not as means all the time, particularly when many serve as means to our personal ends: storekeepers are means of procuring our dinners; customers are means of earning our livelihoods; employees are means of staffing our factories. Both formulations of the Categorical Imperative have to be filled in with the Utilitarian principle—I should want some rule to be a universal law if the consequences of its adoption would be beneficial to others— or with some other values—justice, freedom, etc.—that summarize whole areas of moral conviction. But that principle and those values have to come from outside of the formal Universalist theory.

DISTRIBUTIVE JUSTICE

Neither of the two classical theories, Utilitarianism or Universalism, can be used to judge all moral actions under all circumstances, and consequently two modern ethical systems have been developed, based more upon values than upon principles. The first of these, the theory of Distributive Justice, has been proposed by John Rawls, a member of the Harvard faculty, and is explicitly based upon the primacy of a single value: justice. Justice is felt to be the first virture of social institutions, as truth is the first virtue of systems of thought. A theory, however useful and complete, has to be rejected or revised if it is found to be untrue; in the same fashion our laws and institutions, no matter how efficient or accepted, must be reformed or abolished if they are unjust.

Professor Rawls proposes that society is an association of individuals who cooperate to advance the good of all. Therefore the society, and the institutions within that society, are marked by conflict as well as by collaboration. The collaboration comes about since individuals recognize that joint actions generate much greater benefits than solitary efforts; the conflict is inherent because people are concerned by the just distribution of those benefits. Each person prefers a greater to a lesser share and proposes a system of distribution to ensure that greater share. These distributive systems can have very different bases: to each person equally, or to each according to his or her need, to his or her effort, to his or her contribution, or to his or her competence. Most modern economic systems make use of all five principles:

public education is, theoretically, distributed equally, while welfare payments are on the basis of need, sales commissions on the basis of effort, public honors on the basis of contribution, and managerial salaries on the basis of competence.

Professor Rawls believes that these assorted distributive systems are unjust. He suggests that the primacy of justice in the basic structure of our society requires greater equality, because free and rational persons, recognizing the obvious benefits of cooperation and concerned about the just distribution of those benefits, would accept social and economic inequalities only if they could be shown to result in compensating benefits for everyone, and particularly for the least advantaged members of society: poor, unskilled, and with native intelligence but no training. According to Rawls, I would not object to your having more of the social and economic benefits than I do, but I would object to working hard, beyond the minimum level of effort required to maintain my present standard of living, just so that you could have more. It is not hard to find evidence of this attitude within our society, so the theory of distributive justice does appear to have some empirical support.

Professor Rawls starts, however, not with our society, but with a "natural state," a hypothetical existence at the beginning of time when people were still ignorant of the exact nature of the differences among them—that is, when no one knew who was the most talented, the most energetic, the most competent. What reciprocal arrangement, he asks, would people under those conditions make for the just distribution of the benefits produced by their cooperation? This is the familiar idea of the social contract, and the basic question is, What principles would free and rational persons, concerned with furthering their own interests yet wishing to maintain their cooperative efforts, adopt as defining the fundamental terms of their association?

They would not select absolute equality in the distribution of benefits, Professor Rawls argues, because they would recognize that some of them would put forth greater efforts, have greater skills, develop greater competences, and so on. They would not agree to absolute inequality based upon effort, skill, or competence because they would not know who among them had those qualities and consequently who among them would receive the greater and the lesser benefits. Instead, they would develop a concept of conditional inequality, where differences in benefits had to be justified, and they would propose a rule that those differences in benefits could be justified only if they could be shown to result in compensating benefits for everyone, and in particular for the least advantaged members of their society. That is, the distribution of income would be unequal, but the inequalities would have to work for the benefit of all, and they would work for the benefit of all by helping in some measure the least advantaged, who would then continue to contribute and cooperate.

Distributive Justice can be expanded from an economic system for the distribution of benefits to an ethical system for the evaluation of behavior in that acts can be considered to be "right" and "just" and "proper" if they lead to greater cooperation by members of our society, and "wrong" and "unjust" and "improper" if they lead in the opposite direction. What are the problems with this concept of distributive justice? It is entirely dependent upon an acceptance of the proposition that social cooperation provides the basis for all economic and social benefits; individual effort is downplayed, if not ignored. We all recognize that some organized activities would never take place unless some one individual was willing to take the risks and responsibilities of starting and directing those activities. This individual effort is ignored in Distributive Justice: it forms the basis, however, for the fifth and last economic system to be discussed.

PERSONAL LIBERTY

The theory of Personal Liberty (this phrase is my own, developed to contrast with Distributive Justice) is an ethical system proposed by Robert Nozick, also currently a member of the Harvard faculty. This system is another based upon the primacy of a single value, rather than a single principle, but that value is liberty rather than justice. Liberty is thought to be the first requirement of society. An institution or law that violates individual liberty, even though it may result in greater happiness and increased benefits for others, has to be rejected as being unjust.

Professor Nozick agrees that society is an association of individuals, and that cooperation between those individuals is necessary for economic gain, but he would argue that the cooperation comes about as a result of the exchange of goods and services. The holdings of each person, in income, wealth, and the other bases of self-respect, are derived from other people in exchange for some good or service, or are received from other people in the form of a gift. An existing pattern of holdings may have come about through application of any of the principles of distribution (to each equally, or to each according to need, effort, contribution, or competence), but those patterns will be changed by transfers, and those transfers, by exchange or gift, can be considered to be "just" as long as they are voluntary. Nonvoluntary exchanges, based upon the use of social force or other coercive means, are unjust.

Personal Liberty can be expanded from essentially a market system for the exchange of holdings to an ethical system for the evaluation of behavior, because individuals must be allowed to make informed choices among alternative courses of action leading toward their own welfare, and these choices are "just" or "right" or "proper" as long as the same opportunities for informed choices are extended to others. Justice depends upon equal opportunities for choice and exchange, not upon equal allocations of wealth and income. What is wrong with this concept of liberty? It is based upon a very narrow definition of liberty that is limited to the negative right not to suffer interference from others; there may also be a positive right to receive some of the benefits enjoyed by others. That is, the right to life is certainly the right not to be killed by your neighbors, but it may also include the right to continue living through access to some minimal level of food, shelter, clothing, and medical assistance. And, it is assumed that the food, shelter, clothing, and medical assistance are produced through personal initiative, not through social cooperation.

CONCLUSIONS ON NORMATIVE PHILOSOPHY AS THE BASIS FOR MORAL CHOICE

There are five major ethical systems, as summarized in Exhibit 4–1. They do not outwardly conflict with each other—an action such as lying that is considered immoral in one system will generally be considered immoral in all the other systems—but they

EXHIBIT 4–1 _____
Summary of Beliefs and Problems in the Five Major Ethical Systems

	Nature of the Ethical Belief	_Problems in the Ethical System_
Eternal Law	Moral standards are given in an Eternal Law, which is revealed in Scripture or apparent in nature and then interpreted by religious leaders or humanist philosophers; the belief is that everyone should act in accordance with the interpretation.	There are multiple interpretations of the Law, but no method to choose among them beyond human rationality, and human rationality needs an absolute principle or value as the basis for choice.
Utilitarian Theory	Moral standards are applied to the outcome of an action or decision; the principle is that everyone should act to generate the greatest benefits for the largest number of people.	Immoral acts can be justified if they provide substantial benefits for the majority, even at an unbearable cost or harm to the minority; an additional principle or value is needed to balance the benefit-cost equation.
Universalist Theory	Moral standards are applied to the intent of an action or decision; the principle is that everyone should act to ensure that similar decisions would be reached by others, given similar circumstances.	Immoral acts can be justified by persons who are prone to self-deception or self-importance, and there is no scale to judge between "wills"; an additional principle or value is needed to refine the Categorical Imperative concept.
Distributive Justice	Moral standards are based upon the primacy of a single value, which is justice. Everyone should act to ensure a more equitable distribution of benefits, for this promotes individual self-respect, which is essential for social cooperation.	The primacy of the value of justice is dependent upon acceptance of the proposition that an equitable distribution of benefits ensures social cooperation.
Personal Liberty	Moral standards are based upon the primacy of a single value, which is liberty. Everyone should act to ensure greater freedom of choice, for this promotes market exchange, which is essential for social productivity.	The primacy of the value of liberty is dependent upon acceptance of the proposition that a market system of exchange ensures social productivity.

cannot be reconciled into a logically consistent whole, for eventually conflict will arise over the primacy of the alternative principles and values. Each ethical system expresses a portion of the truth. Each system has adherents and opponents. And each, it is important to admit, is incomplete or inadequate as a means of judging the moral content of individual actions or decisions. What does this mean to managers? I would suggest that there is one major implication for managers, and three more minor or indirect consequences for organizations, that come from the incomplete nature of ethical systems.

The major implication for managers is that there is no single system of belief, with rationally derived standards of moral behavior or methods of moral reasoning, that can guide executives fully in reaching difficult ethical decisions. An ethical decision, to repeat the earlier definition and sharpen the present discussion, is one that will affect others in ways that are beyond their control. A decision to introduce a new brand of chocolate cake mix has no ethical dimensions since others within the society are perfectly free to buy or ignore the product. But a decision to close the plant producing the cake mix, or to use a high-cholesterol shortening in the production of that mix, or to ask for government help in shutting off imports, would have an ethical content, since these issues do have an impact upon others. A product manager, faced, let us say in an unlikely but perhaps not totally unrealistic problem, with imported cake mixes from a foreign country that has very low wage rates and very high government subsidies, has to respond, and each response has ethical implications. Lowering production means cutting employment; reducing the cost means compromising the quality; and requesting government help means endorsing trade restrictions.

There is no single system of belief to guide managers in reaching difficult ethical decisions, but this does not mean that all of us are on our own, to do as we like in our decisions and actions that affect others. We do have obligations to others. We cannot ignore those obligations. The difficulty comes in identifying our obligations and then in evaluating our alternatives, with no single set of moral standards to guide us.

What should we do? Instead of using just one ethical system, which we must admit is imperfect, we have to use all five systems and think through the consequences of our actions on multiple dimensions. Does a given decision result in greater benefits than damages for society as a whole, not just for our organization as part of that society? Is the decision self-serving, or would we be willing to have everyone else take the same action when faced with the same circumstances? We understand the need for social cooperation; will our decision increase or decrease the willingness of others to contribute? We recognize the importance of personal freedom; will our decision increase or decrease the liberty of others to act? Last, we know that the universe is large and infinite, while we are small and our lives are short; is our personal improvement that important, measured against the immensity of that other scale?[4]

Moral reasoning of this nature, utilizing all five ethical systems, is not simple and easy, but it is satisfying. It does work. It works particularly well when combined with economic and legal analysis. That combination will be the topic of the next chapter, Managerial Ethics and Individual Decisions.

Notes

1. For a more complete discussion of the very basic question of ethical relativism, see Richard Brand, *Ethical Theory* (New York: Prentice-Hall, 1959).

2. Albert Carr, in a controversial article ("Is Business Bluffing Ethical?" *Harvard Business Review*, January–February 1968), suggested that business is a game, and that it is necessary only to follow the rules of the game, not personal moral standards.

3. It seems awkward to discuss the philosophic basis of religious belief in a book on management, but religious beliefs do have an impact upon managers as well as upon others and should be included in any description of ethical systems.

4. Once again I am faced with the problem of discussing religious beliefs in a book on management, with the added complexity of recognizing that these beliefs differ among the major religious groups in the United States. Rather than use the moral standards of one group as representative of all others, I prefer to refer to the immensity of the concept of an Eternal Law and let each faith infer its own standards based upon an interpretation of that law.

CASES

Five Moral Problems for Resolution

The following are five short moral problems. They can be classi-fied as moral problems rather than business decisions because someone is going to be hurt or harmed in some way regardless of the final choice. For example if you decide that it is "right" to market radar detectors (the first problem described below), then there probably will be higher speeds, greater accidents, and more deaths and injuries; if you decide that it is "wrong" to market those units, then you are definitely interfering with the rights of others to choose for themselves in a free society.

1. *Selling radar detectors.* Radar detectors, also known as "fuzz-busters," are simple but extremely sensitive radio receivers that are tuned to the wavelength of the police radar. When a car equipped with a detector first enters the radar field, a warning light flashes or a buzzer sounds, enabling the driver to slow down, if necessary, before the speed of the car can be calculated by the police equipment. The use of radar detectors, therefore, enables drivers to avoid being stopped and fined for speeding.

Speeding is alleged to be responsible for 65 percent of all traf-fic accidents. There were 33.8 million traffic accidents in 1987, and those traffic accidents caused 46,400 deaths, 1.8 million se-vere injuries that required hospitalization, 7.8 million moderate injuries that required medical attention, uncounted minor inju-ries, large personal traumas, and huge financial losses.

The use of radar detectors is illegal in many states, but neither the manufacturing nor the marketing of the units has ever been banned by the federal government which, of course, is the sole authority which could regulate their interstate trade. Question: Is it "right" for a company to make and sell radar detectors?

2. *Changing corporate pensions.* In the spring of 1990, General Motors announced that it was planning to change the pension pol-icies affecting its senior executives. In the past, each pension had been calculated as a percentage of the last three years' average salary payments. In the future, the pension would be a percentage of the last three years' average salary *plus* bonus payments. The bonus payments for senior executives at General Motors tend to equal or exceed their salaries; consequently the effect of this policy change would be to double or more than double the pension benefits for a limited number of people. As an example, the pension for Roger Smith, chairman of General Motors, was expected to increase from $550,000 per year to $1,150,000.

The decision to increase the pension benefits for senior executives occurred at a time when the company was also planning to reduce the pension benefits paid to midlevel retirees. Alarmed by the rapid increase in health-care costs, General Motors had notified 84,000 former salaried employees that their health-care coverage was being substantially lowered. The company was legally able to change provisions of the retirement coverage because those provisions had never been part of a written contract. Question: Is it "right" for the company to substantially increase the future pension payments of current senior executives and substantially decrease the health-care coverage of retired midlevel managers?

3. *Cutting old-growth timber.* In 1985, the Pacific Lumber Company of Scotia, California, was the largest private owner of redwood timberland in the United States and a firm that was widely respected by most environmentalists. The company had followed conservative logging practices since its founding in the late 1890s, never clear-cutting the land but always leaving some of the older trees to provide shade and protection for the new seedlings. The result was that the company was on a "sustained yield" basis, cutting slightly less than the annual growth each year, and the timberland was considered to be in excellent condition.

In 1982, the grandson of the founder of Pacific Lumber Company died suddenly, leaving children too young to take over the management of the firm. A new group of managers was brought in, and they continued the traditional logging practices even though earnings remained lower than at most other timber companies on the West Coast—due, it was said, to the high cost of selective cutting. Some of the family's stock in the company was sold to pay estate taxes, and the new management group sold additional shares to raise money for debt repayment.

The family holdings of company stock were then less than 30 percent, and in 1985, Mr. Charles Hurwitz, who had made both a reputation and a fortune as a corporate raider, offered to buy the majority of the shares on the open market. The new management group fought Mr. Hurwitz's early efforts, but when he raised his bid to $700 million, financed by high-return, high-risk junk bonds, they were unable to compete and surrendered control.

To pay off the debt, the new owner quadrupled the rate of harvesting on company lands, clear-cutting the timber and ending the traditional practice of sustained yield logging. A forest survey just before the sale of the company showed a total value of $1.8 billion in redwood timber; at the new rate of harvesting all of that would be gone in 18 years. Question: Is it "right" for a new owner to clear-cut timber that had been preserved by the prior owners for nearly 100 years?

4. *Pricing essential drugs.* In 1987, azidothymidine (AZT) was the only drug that seemed to be effective against the acquired immunodeficiency syndrome (AIDS). AZT blocks the reproduction of the AIDS virus within the bloodstream of the victim, thereby stabilizing the condition of the patient. AZT does not cure AIDS. It does, however, enable the patient in nonadvanced cases to continue living in the hope that a cure will be found.

AZT was developed by the Burroughs Wellcome Company, in cooperation with the federal government. Burroughs Wellcome is a midsize pharmaceutical company based in North Carolina. It is completely owned by Wellcome Ltd., which is a charitable trust located in Great Britain.

AZT was first synthesized in very minute amounts by a government-funded scientist at the National Cancer Institute in 1964. At the time, it was felt that cancer might be a viral disease, and the drug was developed as a defense against viral infections. AZT was found to be ineffective in blocking the spread of cancer cells, and consequently it was neglected for the next 20 years. In 1984, a scientist at Burroughs Wellcome heard of the earlier effort, tried the drug against AIDS in laboratory animals, and found that it worked. The next five years were spent developing the production process (which is exceedingly complex in order to ensure the purity that is needed), conducting human trials, gaining regulatory approval, and starting the marketing process.

The drug is now being offered for sale at a retail price of $1.80 per tablet. The problem is that the typical patient requires 12 tablets per day, which amounts to $7,800 per year. An unfortunate paradox is that many of the 78,000 people diagnosed with the AIDS virus have no health insurance. Consequently, many are unable to pay for the drug that will prolong their lives.

Burroughs Wellcome has consistently refused to divulge precise cost data on the drug, but it does say that it is following pricing polices that are traditional in the pharmaceutical industry. Under those traditional policies, the manufactured cost (material, labor, and factory overhead) would be about 50 cents per tablet and the wholesale price, $1.50. Administrative expenses, liability insurance, and future research and development would not be included in the manufactured cost estimate. Question: Should a drug company follow traditional pricing policies, given that the resulting prices will make a given drug unaffordable to some dying patients?

5. Making political contributions. In 1989, it was revealed that five U.S. senators had received approximately $1.8 million in campaign contributions from Charles Keating, chairman of Lincoln Savings and Loan, Inc., of Orange County, California, during 1988, an election year. The donations were not technically campaign contributions. It is illegal for a single person or single company to donate more than $10,000 to the political campaign of a single candidate in a single year. Instead, the money had been given to political causes that were expected to help the senators in their home states. $900,000 had gone to a campaign to register voters in California, for example. All of the funds were then spent to register voters in heavily Democratic districts, which of course was beneficial to Senator Cranston, Democrat of California, one of the five who received the money.

In 1988, Lincoln Savings and Loan was undergoing a lengthy investigation by the federal government, which alleged improper loans and impending bankruptcy. The five senators met as a group with the regulators involved in the investigation on two separate occasions during that year and urged caution and delay. In defense of the senators, it should be explained that the national accounting firm retained by Lincoln and numerous economic consultants employed by Lincoln claimed that the savings and loan was not bankrupt and that the ongoing investigation appeared to be simply a personal vendetta against Mr. Keating by government officials.

Lincoln Savings and Loan did become insolvent in early 1989, and the company was then taken over by the government. At that time it was announced that the repayment of the federally insured depositors would cost the government (and consequently the taxpayers) $2 billion. The five senators have continually claimed that they did "nothing wrong". There are two questions in this case: Was it "right" for Lincoln Savings and Loan to make large but legal campaign contributions to members of the U.S. Senate? Was it "right" for the members of the Senate to accept those contributions, and then intercede with the regulators on behalf of the donor?

Class Assignment.   Decide in your own mind what is "right" and what is "wrong" in these five short moral problems that need resolution. They are not simple problems. It is suggested that you make use of the four methods of moral reasoning described in the text of Chapter 4 and summarized below:

1. Utilitarianism states that it is the outcome of a decision or action that is important, for it is the result that truly matters in our treatment of other people. The principle to be followed is that of beneficiency: A decision or action is "right" only if it generates the greatest amount of benefit at the lowest cost or harm of any of the alternatives.

2. Universalism states that it is the intent of a decision or action that is important, for we can never accurately foresee and evaluate all of the possible results. The principle to be followed is consistency: A decision or action is "right" only if we could will that everyone, faced with the same set of circumstances, should make the same decision or take the same action.

3. Distributive Justice is based upon the primacy of a single value rather than a single principle, and that value is justice. A belief in the primacy of justice leads us to select decisions and actions as "right" only if the least advantaged members of our society somehow enjoy a better standard of living after the decision or action than they did before.

4. Personal Liberty is also based upon the primacy of a single value rather than a single principle, but in this case that value is

liberty. A belief in the primacy of liberty leads us to select decisions and actions as "right" only if all members of our society somehow have a greater freedom to develop their own lives in their own way after the decision or action than they did before.

Tuna, Dolphins, and H. J. Heinz

Assume that you have just started work at the H. J. Heinz Company. Heinz, if you are not familiar with the firm, is a large food products company, headquartered in Pittsburgh, and was one of the first to become active in international manufacturing and marketing. Over one half of the company's sales revenues now comes from outside the United States.

Assume that you were very pleased to receive a job offer from Heinz. It is a rapidly growing company with numerous opportunities for younger managers. Further, it tends to recruit very few business students, and then only for positions in international marketing and finance. Domestic positions have traditionally been filled by promotion from within the company.

Assume finally that at the end of your first week on the job you and the approximately 25 other recent graduates of business schools and law schools in both the United States and Europe who were part of the training program were invited to a reception to meet Mr. A. J. H. O'Reilly, the chairman of Heinz.

You were particularly pleased to have an opportunity to meet Mr. O'Reilly. He has an unusual reputation in business circles. He is a native of Ireland and still maintains his home in that country, flying to Pittsburgh (headquarters for the global corporation and the U.S. division), London (headquarters of the European division), and Sidney, Australia (headquarters for the Pacific division). He is an urbane, sophisticated man who attempts to keep a low profile in the business press. A number of years ago, he was quoted as saying that the function of a chairman is to set a clear direction and explicit goals for the company, select good people to achieve those goals, and then keep well out of their way. The phrase *keep well out of their way* seemed to appeal to the media.

Numerous magazines published pictures of Mr. O'Reilly salmon fishing on his estate in Ireland or riding in a fox hunt across the picturesque Irish landscape, under that title. Mr. O'Reilly simply ignored those jibes that implied that he works very little. He could afford to do so. H. J. Heinz had increased its earnings substantially each year for the 17 years that he had been chairman.

In addition to the unusual reputation in business circles, Mr. O'Reilly has an unusual background, which includes an undergraduate degree in Moral Philosophy from Dublin College, a Ph.D. in Economics from Bradford University, and a law degree from the University of Paris. He was appointed president of Heinz at age 37, after 10 years as first a marketing executive and then general manager of the very successful European division.

At the reception, Mr. O'Reilly talked to your group about his view of a truly global economy, bound together by rapid advances in telecommunication technologies and equally rapid changes in consumer preferences. He finished by describing his vision of the future of H. J. Heinz as part of that economy, that technology, and that market. It was not a mundane address. It obviously reflected his deeply held beliefs. He then circulated around the room, guided by the vice president of personnel, who introduced each recent hiree with a brief comment about that person's interests or background. For example, the person standing next to you happened to be from the University of Paris, and Mr. O'Reilly said a few words about the days when he was a student at that university.

When it was your turn, the vice president introduced you by name, and then explained that you had taken a course in ethics at your university. You wondered why he had picked upon such a minor portion of your background, but Mr. O'Reilly was immediately interested. He asked about the content in the course. You described the sequence of looking at economics, the law, and then moral philosophy as different determinants of what is right, and then stopped, for you wondered just how much detail he wanted. He nodded his head and said, "Yes, yes, do go on," so you completed the listing with Mill, Kant, Rawls, and Nozick. He asked you to comment on Kant's Second Formulation of the Categorical Imperative (treat each person as an end, valuable in himself or herself, not as a means to an end), which you were very happy to realize you remembered in some detail. He asked which side of the debate between Rawls (who believes that justice is the primary good or goal for society) and Nozick (who takes the opposite side, that freedom is more important than justice) you were on. You responded.

It seemed as if he were testing your knowledge of the basic concepts and your understanding of the first principles. He appeared satisfied, however, for he nodded his head and said, "Exactly" or "Of course" a number of times as you spoke. He chatted for a few more minutes about his own thoughts upon the latter subject (Rawls vs. Nozick) and about his belief that modern managers should have a better understanding of what he termed "the moral and political economy of business."

Then, he turned to the vice president of personnel and said, "Susan, I should like to borrow this young person for a few days next week, if you can spare him (her) from the training program for that period of time." There was, of course, rapid agreement from the vice president. Mr. O'Reilly then turned back to you and explained that he would like you to write a short report addressed to him explaining what H. J. Heinz should do relative to the killing and maiming of dolphins that seemed to be an unavoidable consequence of fishing for tuna. Starkist tuna, you already knew from one of the introductory lectures about the company, was one of the major brands produced by the firm, and accounted for 9 percent of sales and 11 percent of profits. "Don't tell me what you think I want to hear," was his parting comment as he went on to talk with others in the room. "Tell me what you think the company ought to do." He emphasized the word *ought*. Then he finished by saying, "Give the report to my secretary next Wednesday. If you tell people in the company you are working for me, I feel fairly certain that you will be able to get the background information you will need. Susan (the personnel vice president) can help you get started."

You spent the weekend learning as much as you could about commercial tuna fishing from reports accumulated by the staff of the personnel vice president. You found that the basic facts were depressingly familiar to everyone who wrote on the subject. The best tuna is termed *albacore*, and it comes from the eastern tropics of the Pacific, a 6-million-square-mile area that extends between 200 and 600 miles off the coast from northern Chile to southern California.

There is also an Atlantic species of the fish, which is termed *horse mackerel* (due to its larger size than the standard Atlantic mackerel). Horse mackerel is of much lower quality (an oilier and coarser consistency) than albacore tuna. There is a second Pacific species termed *white tuna*, which is found only in the western tropics of the Pacific, but that is heavily fished by the Pacific nations, including Japan, Taiwan, and Indonesia. Finally, there used to be a Mediterranean species called *yellow tuna*, but that has been largely depleted by overfishing.

Albacore tuna are large fish, ranging in size from 15 to 35 pounds. They swim in schools, feeding on the small shrimp and brine minnows that thrive in the warm waters of the eastern tropical Pacific. The Humboldt Current, which is a cold water current from the Antarctic, flows directly along the coasts of South and Central America, and brings nutrients that mix with the warmer waters of the Pacific. The result is a very prolific spawning ground for a wide variety of commercial fish and marine mammals.

Commercial fishing is very active in the area, which is outside the territorial waters of any of the countries along the coast. Fishing fleets come from Italy and Spain in Europe, Japan and Korea in Asia, and most of the American nations.

The problem that arises in commercial fishing for albacore tuna is that, for reasons that are not at all understood despite extensive research by oceanographic scientists, the schools of this species of tuna tend to congregate directly under herds of dolphins. It may be that the tuna and the dolphins are attracted by the same food sources or by the same water temperatures. It may be that a symbiotic (helping) relationship exists between the two species. It remains a fact that albacore tuna are seldom found in large numbers, in the entire 6 million square miles of the eastern tropics of the Pacific, if they are not associated in some way with herds of dolphins.

Dolphins, of course, are mammals, not fish. They have a reputation of being highly intelligent and are able to communicate with one another through a series of squeaks, grunts and whistles. They also have a reputation of being highly playful, often riding the bow waves of boats or leaping over ocean waves in an apparent game of follow the leader. They have even been known to play tag with swimmers along the coast, which can be unnerving for the swimmer but is apparently fun for the dolphin.

Fishing boat captains locate schools of tuna by finding herds of dolphins playing or feeding on the surface. In the earlier methods of fishing, called hand lining, the presence of the dolphins caused no problem. Lines, with baited hooks, were dropped to the level of the tuna, and the fish were reeled in by hand. Modern methods of fishing make use of floating nets, called purse seines, that are up to three miles long and perhaps 100 feet deep. The nets are laid to encircle the visible dolphins and the invisible tuna (though the presence of schools of tuna can now be confirmed by underwater sonar) and pulled tight. The dolphins could easily leap over the floating buoys and cables that support the net, but they seem to become confused, swim in circles, and finally are either suffocated (dolphins are air-breathing mammals) when trapped in the nets or crushed as the nets are hauled aboard the boats by mechanical winches.

In 1972, during the early days of the environmental movement, Congress passed the Marine Mammal Protection Act, which regulated the killing of dolphins in purse seine nets (so named because they look like an old-fashioned string purse, with a single opening at the bottom). The act set a maximum number of dolphins that could be killed per year, and that number was to decline over time from 320,000 in 1972 to 20,000 in 1987.

The Marine Mammal Protection Act applied only to U.S.-registered fishing boats. Most U.S.-registered boats, though not those owned or under contract to H. J. Heinz, simply changed their registry to Mexico, Panama, or Peru. H. J. Heinz attempted to find a means of complying with the law. It used speedboats within the circle of the net, immediately after it was first laid, to chase dolphins and attempt to force them to jump over the supporting buoys and cables. The dolphins ignored the speedboats, or seemed to consider them part of an enjoyable game designed for their amusement, while the tuna were irritated by the propeller sounds and dived under the net. Small explosive charges were tried, with equally discouraging results.

The United States negotiated treaties with other countries active in tuna fishing, attempting to place foreign boats under the same restrictions as the remaining ships in the U.S. fleet. Unfortunately, no observers were permitted on foreign boats, and consequently the negotiated restrictions were said to have been largely ignored. The result was that the dolphin population within the eastern tropics of the Pacific Ocean began to decline rapidly.

You found that in 1989, H. J. Heinz operated within the law; it was the only company to contract with the U.S.-registered boats and thus was "entitled" to the full U.S.-approved kill (20,000 per year) for those boats. Foreign boats have their own approved kill levels, allocated per nation agreeing to the treaty. H. J. Heinz, however, bore the major brunt of the public opposition, partially because it reports the estimated kill each year (as required by U.S. law) but also because two years ago a representative of an environmental group (Greenpeace) signed onto one of the company's boats as a crew member and took surreptitious videotapes of the killing and maiming of dolphins. These videotapes were considered too distressing to be shown on U.S. television, but they were shown on television in many parts of Europe, which started a boycott of the company's canned tuna products. The boycott has not been economically effective—sales of the Starkist canned tuna continue to increase each year both in the U.S. and in Europe—but there was a general agreement that it did not help to build the overall image and reputation of the company.

In short, you found that H. J. Heinz was the only food products company selling tuna in the United States that was actively obeying the U.S. law against killing dolphins, yet it was also the prime target by environmental groups for that killing. And, despite the apparently misdirected anger of the environmental groups, it was necessary to admit that the company did cause the deaths of approximately 20,000 dolphins each year.

There were five basic alternatives beyond the obvious effort to discover a new means of either luring or chasing the dolphins playing on the surface away from the tuna feeding at greater depths. H. J. Heinz had spent $2.5 million supporting oceanographic research, but up to 1989 without a positive result. Some of the more ingenious methods involved broadcasting under water. Sound travels well in water (much further than in the air), and the call of a killer whale, the appeal of an amorous dolphin, and the music of a rock group had all been tried. The first frightened the tuna as well as the dolphins, the second attracted only a very few of the dolphins, and the last apparently was enjoyed by both species. The more serious alternatives open to the company are as follows:

1. Continue commercial fishing for albacore tuna in the eastern Pacific, using U.S. boats with the purse seine technology. The U.S. boats are large, expensive, and efficient; they are able to land tuna in the United States for canning at a cost equal to that of any of the foreign boats. The advantage of this alternative is that the company would remain cost-competitive and have access to the highest grade of tuna. The disadvantage is that the dolphin deaths would continue, though at a rate that would be within the legal limits imposed by U.S. law. A public relations campaign could be started to convince the environmentalists that Heinz was the only firm observing those limits and obeying that law, though of course the success of such a public relations campaign could not be guaranteed.

2. Continue commercial fishing for albacore tuna in the eastern Pacific, using U.S. boats with the purse seine technology, but sell the tuna in Japan and the other nations of the Far East where albacore tuna is regarded as a premium product and may be sold at a premium price, and where the killing of dolphins is not regarded as an environmental crime. In 1989, albacore tuna was one of the few packaged food products that could be imported into Japan without encountering restrictive trade practices. Indeed, the dolphins that were killed as a result of this fishing could also be exported to Japan and the other nations of the Far East as pet food. The advantage of this alternative is that it would generate by far the highest profit for the company and would probably end the boycott. The disadvantage is that it would not end the killing of dolphins.

3. Continue commercial fishing for albacore tuna in the eastern Pacific, using U.S. boats with a hand-line technology. Hand-line fishing with baited hooks in a school of tuna can be a semi-efficient method; the fish are caught quickly but at a considerably higher labor cost. There are numerous advantages to this alternative. The U.S. boats could be converted to this older technology, since the crane used to position and lift the nets could be used to launch and recover the dories, which are small, seaworthy power boats needed for hand-line fishing. The disadvantage is that hand-line fishing would cost about 35 percent more per pound of tuna. Customers could be asked to pay this premium (estimated to add 25 cents to the price of a typical 6-ounce tin) for "dolphin-free" tuna. Or workers from the poverty stricken cities of South America could be hired to man the dories at much lower wages. A problem with the second alternative is that those workers would not be experienced at sea. Fishing from small boats, even when supported by a large mother ship, is considered to be dangerous for inexperienced persons. The new workers could be trained, of course, but it is not certain that trained but inexperienced seamen would react properly in emergencies, such as a sudden storm that caught them in their dories.

4. Change to fishing for white tuna in the western Pacific, using foreign boats and the purse seine technology. Herds of dolphins are seldom associated with schools of tuna in the western Pacific, again for a reason that is not understood. It would therefore be possible to catch dolphin-free tuna. There seem to be few advantages to this alternative, however, beyond that ability. The disadvantages are numerous. The U.S. boats that have fished exclusively for Heinz over the past 20 years could not continue; they do not have large enough fuel tanks to reach the western Pacific, nor large enough refrigerated holds to carry the catch back to the United States. The U.S. canneries, which employ over 2,000 people in southern California, would have to be closed. Foreign canneries, which tend to be less conscientious in quality control, would have to be opened. And, it is thought that foreign fishing fleets that did not observe the U.S. law would simply replace the U.S. boats in the eastern Pacific and kill many more dolphins.

5. Discontinue the production and marketing of canned tuna. As mentioned earlier, in 1989, canned tuna accounted for 9 percent of sales and 11 percent of profits of H. J. Heinz.

Class Assignment. Prepare a recommendation on the future of the Starkist canned tuna product line for the chairman of H. J. Heinz. Obviously, you can select any alternative that you believe to be right, ranging from ignoring the dolphin problem to discontinuing the tuna product, but you should state as clearly as possible why you believe that course of action to be correct. Accept the recommendation of Mr. O'Reilly that you not tell him what you think he wants to hear; instead, tell him what you think is the right thing for the company to do.

The Parable of the Sadhu

Last year, as the first participant in the new six-month sabbatical program that Morgan Stanley has adopted, I enjoyed a rare opportunity to collect my thoughts as well as do some traveling. I spent the first three months in Nepal, walking 600 miles through 200 villages in the Himalayas and climbing some 120,000 vertical feet. On the trip my sole Western companion was an anthropologist who shed light on the cultural patterns of the villages we passed through.

During the Nepal hike, something occured that has had a powerful impact on my thinking about corporate ethics. Although some might argue that the experience has no relevance to business, it was a situation in which a basic ethical dilemma suddenly intruded into the lives of a group of individuals. How the group responded I think holds a lesson for all organizations no matter how defined.

THE SADHU

The Nepal experience was more rugged and adventuresome than I had anticipated. Most commercial treks last two or three weeks and cover a quarter of the distance we traveled.

My friend Stephen, the anthropologist, and I were halfway through the 60-day Himalayan part of the trip when we reached the high point, an 18,000-foot pass over a crest that we'd have to

SOURCE: Bowen H. McCoy, reprinted from *Harvard Business Review*, September–October 1983. Copyright © 1983 by the President and Fellows of Harvard College.

traverse to reach to the village of Muklinath, an ancient holy place for pilgrims.

Six years earlier I had suffered pulmonary edema, an acute form of altitude sickness, at 16,500 feet in the vicinity of Everest base camp, so we were understandably concerned about what would happen at 18,000 feet. Moreover, the Himalayas were having their wettest spring in 20 years; hip-deep powder and ice had already driven us off one ridge. If we failed to cross the pass, I feared that the last half of our "once in a lifetime" trip would be ruined.

The night before we would try the pass, we camped at a hut at 14,500 feet. In the photos taken at that camp, my face appears wan. The last village we'd passed through was a sturdy two-day walk below us, and I was tired.

During the late afternoon, four backpackers from New Zealand joined us, and we spent most of the night awake, anticipating the climb. Below we could see the fires of two other parties, which turned out to be two Swiss couples and a Japanese hiking club.

To get over the steep part of the climb before the sun melted the steps cut in the ice, we departed at 3:30 A.M. The New Zealanders left first, followed by Stephen and myself, our porters and Sherpas, and then the Swiss. The Japanese lingered in their camp. The sky was clear, and we were confident that no spring storm would erupt that day to close the pass.

At 15,500 feet, it looked to me as if Stephen were shuffling and staggering a bit, which are symptoms of altitude sickness. (The initial stage of altitude sickness brings a headache and nausea. As the condition worsens, a climber may encounter difficult breathing, disorientation, aphasia, and paralysis.) I felt strong, my adrenaline was flowing, but I was very concerned about my ultimate ability to get across. A couple of our porters were also suffering from the height, and Pasang, our Sherpa sirdar (leader), was worried.

Just after daybreak, while we rested at 15,500 feet, one of the New Zealanders, who had gone ahead, came staggering down toward us with a body slung across his shoulders. He dumped the almost naked, barefoot body of an Indian holy man—a sadhu—at my feet. He had found the pilgrim lying on the ice, shivering and suffering from hypothermia. I cradled the sadhu's head and laid him out on the rocks. The New Zealander was angry. He wanted to get across the pass before the bright sun melted the snow. He said, "Look, I've done what I can. You have porters and Sherpa guides. You care for him. We're going on!" He turned and went back up the mountain to join his friends.

I took a carotid pulse and found that the sadhu was still alive. We figured he had probably visited the holy shrines at Muklinath and was on his way home. It was fruitless to question why he had chosen this desperately high route instead of the safe, heavily traveled caravan route through the Kali Gandaki gorge. Or why he was almost naked and with no shoes, or how long he had been lying in the pass. The answers weren't going to solve our problem.

Stephen and the four Swiss began stripping off outer clothing and opening their packs. The sadhu was soon clothed from head to foot. He was not able to walk, but he was very much alive. I looked down the mountain and spotted below the Japanese climbers marching up with a horse.

Without a great deal of thought, I told Stephen and Pasang that I was concerned about withstanding the heights to come and wanted to get over the pass. I took off after several of our porters who had gone ahead.

On the steep part of the ascent where, if the ice steps had given way, I would have slid down about 3,000 feet, I felt vertigo. I stopped for a breather, allowing the Swiss to catch up with me. I inquired about the sadhu and Stephen. They said that the sadhu was fine and that Stephen was just behind. I set off again for the summit.

Stephen arrived at the summit an hour after I did. Still exhila-rated by victory, I ran down the snow slope to congratulate him. He was suffering from altitude sickness, walking 15 steps, then stopping, walking 15 steps, then stopping. Pasang accompanied him all the way up. When I reached them, Stephen glared at me and said: "How do you feel about contributing to the death of a fellow man?"

I did not fully comprehend what he meant.

"Is the sadhu dead?" I inquired.

"No," replied Stephen, "but he surely will be!"

After I had gone, and the Swiss had departed not long after, Stephen had remained with the sadhu. When the Japanese had arrived, Stephen had asked to use their horse to transport the sadhu down to the hut. They had refused. He had then asked Pasang to have a group of our porters carry the sadhu. Pasang had resisted the idea, saying that the porters would have to exert all their energy to get themselves over the pass. He had thought they could not carry a man down 1,000 feet to the hut, reclimb the slope, and get across safely before the snow melted. Pasang had pressed Stephen not to delay any longer.

The Sherpas had carried the sadhu down to a rock in the sun at about 15,000 feet and had pointed out the hut another 500 feet below. The Japanese had given him food and drink. When they had last seen him he was listlessly throwing rocks at the Japanese party's dog, which had frightened him.

We do not know if the sadhu lived or died.

For many of the following days and evenings Stephen and I discussed and debated our behavior toward the sadhu. Stephen is a committed Quaker with deep moral vision. He said, "I feel that what happened with the sadhu is a good example of the breakdown between the individual ethic and the corporate ethic. No one person was willing to assume ultimate responsibility for the sadhu. Each was willing to do his bit just so long as it was not too inconvenient. When it got to be a bother, everyone just passed the buck to someone else and took off. Jesus was relevant to a more individualistic stage of society, but how do we interpret his teaching today in a world filled with large, impersonal organizations and groups?"

I defended the larger group, saying, "Look, we all cared. We all stopped and gave aid and comfort. Everyone did his bit. The New Zealander carried him down below the snow line. I took his pulse and suggested we treat him for hypothermia. You and the Swiss gave him clothing and got him warmed up. The Japanese gave him food and water. The Sherpas carried him down to the sun and pointed out the easy trail toward the hut. He was well enough to throw rocks at a dog. What more could we do?"

"You have just described the typical affluent Westerner's response to a problem. Throwing money—in this case food and sweaters—at it, but not solving the fundamentals!" Stephen retorted.

"What would satisfy you?" I said. "Here we are, a group of New Zealanders, Swiss, Americans, and Japanese who have never met before and who are at the apex of one of the most powerful experiences of our lives. Some years the pass is so bad no one gets over it. What right does an almost naked pilgrim who chooses the wrong trail have to disrupt our lives? Even the Sherpas had no interest in risking the trip to help him beyond a certain point."

Stephen calmly rebutted, "I wonder what the Sherpas would have done if the sadhu had been a well-dressed Nepali, or what the Japanese would have done if the sadhu had been a well-dressed Asian, or what you would have done, Buzz, if the sadhu had been a well-dressed Western woman?"

"Where, in your opinion," I asked instead, "is the limit of our responsibility in a situation like this? We had our own well-being to worry about. Our Sherpa guides were unwilling to jeopardize us or the porters for the sadhu. No one else on the mountain was willing to commit himself beyond certain self-imposed limits."

Stephen said, "As individual Christians or people with a Western ethical tradition, we can fulfill our obligations in such a situation only if (1) the sadhu dies in our care, (2) the sadhu demonstrates to us that he could undertake the two-day walk down to the village, or (3) we carry the sadhu for two days down to the village and convince someone there to care for him."

"Leaving the sadhu in the sun with food and clothing, while he demonstrated hand-eye coordination by throwing a rock at a dog, comes close to fulfilling items one and two," I answered. "And it wouldn't have made sense to take him to the village where the people appeared to be far less caring than the Sherpas, so the third condition is impractical. Are you really saying that, no matter what the implications, we should, at the drop of a hat, have changed our entire plan?"

THE INDIVIDUAL VERSUS THE GROUP ETHIC

Despite my arguments, I felt and continue to feel guilt about the sadhu. I had literally walked through a classic moral dilemma without fully thinking through the consequences. My excuses for my actions include a high adrenaline flow, a superordinate goal, and a once-in-a-lifetime opportunity—factors in the usual corporate situation, especially when one is under stress.

Real moral dilemmas are ambiguous, and many of us hike right through them, unaware that they exist. When, usually after the fact, someone makes an issue of them, we tend to resent his or her bringing it up. Often, when the full import of what we have done (or not done) falls on us, we dig into a defensive position from which it is very difficult to emerge. In rare circumstances we may contemplate what we have done from inside a prison.

Had we mountaineers been free of physical and mental stress caused by the effort and the high altitude, we might have treated the sadhu differently. Yet isn't stress the real test of personal and corporate values? The instant decisions executives make under pressure reveal the most about personal and corporate character.

Among the many questions that occur to me when pondering my experience are: What are the practical limits of moral imagination and vision? Is there a collective or institutional ethic beyond the ethics of the individual? At what level of effort or commitment can one discharge one's ethical responsibilities?

Not every ethical dilemma has a right solution. Reasonable people often disagree; otherwise there would be no dilemma. In a business context, however, it is essential that managers agree on a process for dealing with dilemmas.

The sadhu experience offers an interesting parallel to business situations. An immediate response was mandatory. Failure to act was a decision in itself. Up on the mountain we could not resign and submit our résumés to a headhunter. In contrast to philosophy, business involves action and implementation—getting things done. Managers must come up with answers to problems based on what they see and what they allow to influence their decision-making processes. On the mountain, none of us but Stephen realized the true dimensions of the situation we were facing.

One of our problems was that as a group we had no process for developing a consensus. We had no sense of purpose or plan. The difficulties of dealing with the sadhu were so complex that no one person could handle it. Because it did not have a set of preconditions that could guide its action to an acceptable resolution, the group reacted instinctively as individuals. The cross-cultural nature of the group added a further layer of complexity. We had no leader with whom we could all identify and in whose purpose we believed. Only Stephen was willing to take charge, but he could not gain adequate support to care for the sadhu.

Some organizations do have a value system that transcends the personal values of the managers. Such values, which go beyond profitability, are usually revealed when the organization is under stress. People throughout the organization generally accept its values, which, because they are not presented as a rigid list of commandments, may be somewhat ambiguous. The stories people tell, rather than printed materials, transmit these conceptions of what is proper behavior.

For 20 years I have been exposed at senior levels to a variety of corporations and organizations. It is amazing how quickly an outsider can sense the tone and style of an organization and the degree of tolerated openness and freedom to challenge management.

Organizations that do not have a heritage of mutually accepted, shared values tend to become unhinged during stress, with each individual bailing out for himself. In the great takeover battles we have witnessed during past years, companies that had strong cultures drew the wagons around them and fought it out, while other companies saw executives, supported by their golden parachutes, bail out of the struggles.

Because corporations and their members are interdependent, for the corporation to be strong the members need to share a preconceived notion of what is correct behavior, a "business ethic," and think of it as a positive force, not a constraint.

As an investment banker I am continually warned by well-meaning lawyers, clients, and associates to be wary of conflicts of interest. Yet if I were to run away from every difficult situation, I wouldn't be an effective investment banker. I have to feel my way through conflicts. An effective manager can't run from risk either; he or she has to confront and deal with risk. To feel "safe" in doing this, managers need the guidelines of an agreed-on process and set of values within the organization.

After my three months in Nepal, I spent three months as an executive-in-residence at both Stanford Business School and the Center for Ethics and Social Policy at the Graduate Theological Union at Berkeley. These six months away from my job gave me time to assimilate 20 years of business experience. My thoughts turned often to the meaning of the leadership role in any large organization. Students at the seminary thought of themselves as antibusiness. But when I questioned them they agreed that they distrusted all large organizations, including the church. They perceived all large organizations as impersonal and opposed to individual values and needs. Yet we all know of organizations where peoples' values and beliefs are respected and their expressions encouraged. What makes the difference? Can we identify the difference and, as a result, manage more effectively?

The word "ethics" turns off many and confuses more. Yet the notions of shared values and an agreed-on process for dealing with adversity and change—what many people mean when they talk about corporate culture—seem to be at the heart of the ethical issue. People who are in touch with their own core beliefs and the beliefs of others and are sustained by them can be more comfortable living on the cutting edge. At times, taking a tough line or a decisive stand in a muddle of ambiguity is the only ethical thing to do. If a manager is indecisive and spends time trying to figure out the "good" thing to do, the enterprise may be lost.

Business ethics, then, has to do with the authenticity and integrity of the enterprise. To be ethical is to follow the business as well as the cultural goals of the corporation, its owners, its employees, and its customers. Those who cannot serve the corporate vision are not authentic business people and, therefore, are not ethical in the business sense.

At this stage of my own business experience I have a strong interest in organizational behavior. Sociologists are keenly studying what they call corporate stories, legends, and heroes as a way organizations have of transmitting the value system. Corporations such as Arco have even hired consultants to perform an audit of their corporate culture. In a company, the leader is the person who understands, interprets, and manages the corporate value system. Effective managers are then action-oriented people who resolve conflict, are tolerant of ambiguity, stress, and change, and have a strong sense of purpose for themselves and their organizations.

If all this is true, I wonder about the role of the professional manager who moves from company to company. How can he or she quickly absorb the values and culture of different organizations? Or is there, indeed, an art of management that is totally transportable? Assuming such fungible managers do exist, is it proper for them to manipulate the values of others?

What would have happened had Stephen and I carried the sadhu for two days back to the village and become involved with the villagers in his care? In four trips to Nepal my most interesting experiences occurred in 1975 when I lived in a Sherpa home in the Khumbu for five days recovering from altitude sickness. The high point of Stephen's trip was an invitation to participate in a family funeral ceremony in Manang. Neither experience had to do with climbing the high passes of the Himalayas. Why were we so reluctant to try the lower path, the ambiguous trail? Perhaps because we did not have a leader who could reveal the greater purpose of the trip to us.

Why didn't Stephen with his moral vision opt to take the sadhu under his personal care? The answer is because, in part, Stephen was hard-stressed physically himself, and because, in part, without some support system that involved our involuntary and episodic community on the mountain, it was beyond his individual capacity to do so.

I see the current interest in corporate culture and corporate value systems as a positive response to Stephen's pessimism about the decline of the role of the individual in large organizations. Individuals who operate from a thoughtful set of personal values provide the foundation for a corporate culture. A corporate tradition that encourages freedom of inquiry, supports personal values, and reinforces a focused sense of direction can fulfill the need for individuality along with the prosperity and success of the group. Without such corporate support, the individual is lost.

That is the lesson of the sadhu. In a complex corporate situation, the individual requires and deserves the support of the group. If people cannot find such support from their organization, they don't know how to act. If such support is forthcoming, a person has a stake in the success of the group, and can add much to the process of establishing and maintaining a corporate culture. It is management's challenge to be sensitive to individual needs, to shape them, and to direct and focus them for the benefit of the group as a whole.

For each of us the sadhu lives. Should we stop what we are doing and comfort him; or should we keep trudging up toward the high pass? Should I pause to help the derelict I pass on the street each night as I walk by the Yale Club en route to Grand Central Station? Am I his brother? What is the nature of our responsibility if we consider ourselves to be ethical persons? Perhaps it is to change the values of the group so that it can, with all its resources, take the other road.

CHAPTER 5

Managerial Ethics and Individual Decisions

We have looked at economic analysis, legal analysis, and philosophical analysis as means of resolving ethical dilemmas and have found that none is completely satisfactory; none gives us a method of deciding upon a course of action that we can say with certainty is "right" and "proper" and "good" when attempting to find a balance between the economic and the social performance of an organization.

Economic analysis was the first to be investigated. The concept of impersonal market forces helping us to reach Pareto Optimality is appealing—all we have to do, then, is to maximize revenues and minimize costs, and the product markets, factor markets, and political decisions will together eliminate or correct the harm or damages we cause to others. However, there are both practical and theoretical problems with microeconomic theory. We have to admit that markets are not so efficient and that voters are not so generous.

Legal analysis was the next to be considered. The concept of impersonal social processes is also appealing—all we have to do is to obey the law and we can feel that we are meeting the collective moral standards of a majority of our population—but that falls apart as we look at the process by which individual norms, beliefs, and values are institutionalized into the legal framework. We have to recognize that there are too many steps and too many compromises between individual moral standards and national legal requirements.

Philosophical analysis was the last to be reviewed. The concept of personal rational analysis is appealing—all we have to do is base our decisions upon a single principle (beneficiency or consistency) or upon a single value (justice or freedom)—but rational analysis has an internal flaw. If we attempt to use any one of the principles or any one of the values in moral reasoning, we find that we have to add a second principle or a second value to reach a logical conclusion. We have to accept that a combination of conflicting principles or values is not rational.

What do we do, then? How do we decide, when faced with an ethical dilemma that contrasts economic performance and social performance? We are forced to use all three methods of analysis.

We are forced to say to ourselves that if one of our decisions or actions generates an adequate financial return, conforms to current law, provides substantial benefits to a large number of people, is an action we can wish that everyone else would take when faced with the same set of alternatives and background factors, is "just" in the sense of increasing the potential for social cooperation, and is "equitable" in the sense of expanding the ability of others to choose for themselves, then we can say that decision or action is "right" and "proper" and "good."

Granted, this form of multiple analysis is complex. It would be better if we had a single decision rule that we could follow every time, but we don't. Does multiple analysis work? Yes, I think that it does. Let me show that it does by following through two examples of foreign bribery, one of which I think most of us would agree to be "wrong" and the other of which I think most of us would agree to be "permissible" if not "right." Let us see whether multiple analysis helps us to understand these intuitive beliefs. If a means of analysis helps us to understand our intuitive beliefs—based upon our personal moral standards—when confronting a reasonably simple ethical problem, then I think that we can place greater reliance upon it when we don't have clear intuitive feelings and we face much more complex ethical issues.

ETHICAL ANALYSIS AND THE LOCKHEED BRIBERY CASE

The first example—and the one that I think we can agree to be intuitively wrong—is that of Lockheed, and the payment of $3.8 million by the Lockheed Aircraft Corporation to various governmental officials and representatives of the prime minister in Japan to ensure the purchase of 20 TriStar passenger planes. This event was extensively reported, following testimony before a congressional investigating committee, and Mr. Carl Kotchian, the president of Lockheed, has written an account of the conditions that led him to decide to pay the bribes. In his defense, I think that we have to understand that Mr. Kotchian did not leave for Japan carrying the corporate checkbook and a ballpoint pen; in essence, he was forced into the payments.

Mr. Kotchian was directly responsible for the negotiations that led to the sale of the TriStar planes. However, he did not speak Japanese and had to rely on advice and representations from the executives of a Japanese trading company that had been retained to act as the agent for Lockheed. I think we can assume that Mr. Kotchian had been prepared by his staff for the personal nature of Japanese business decisions on large-scale investments, which is a corollary of the consensus nature of Japanese business decisions on operating problems—after all, if product design and manufacturing method decisions are made by a group on the lower levels of the organization, the pattern will be established for strategic and investment decisions to be made by a group on the upper levels. I think that we can also assume that Mr. Kotchian had been warned by his staff of the interlocking structure of Japanese business firms and governmental agencies. But, no Westerner can be fully prepared for the intricate maneuvering that this combination of group decision making and interlocking organizational structures can generate.

These maneuvers, which Mr. Kotchian described as "Byzantine" in their complexity, extended over a period of 70 days. While Mr. Kotchian waited in a hotel room in downtown Tokyo, he was exposed to hurried meetings, intentional delays, midnight telephone calls, and continual intimations that the decision was at hand. Being a foreigner and acting as a salesman, Mr. Kotchian was excluded from the decision process. The agents retained by Lockheed could meet with the prime minister at his private home for breakfast, but the president of Lockheed could meet only with the technical and functional representatives of the airlines, who might advise but could not decide upon the purchase. These meetings, delays, and telephone calls were played out against a backdrop of a declining order backlog and a deteriorating competitive position for the company. Lockheed had failed over the prior two years to obtain orders from Alitalia, Lufthansa, and Sabena, in Europe, and a large foreign order was needed to bring unit sales above the break-even volume and repay the engineering expense. The agents for Lockheed calmly assumed that "pledges" would be made and explained that payments would be required to ensure the sale of 20 planes to Nippon, in Japan. Perhaps Mr. Kotchian wondered, as he sat in that hotel room waiting for the next meeting or the next telephone call, if other aircraft suppliers had made those pledges in Europe, for the Tri-Star was an acceptable design, certainly equal to the competition. Probably he worried about the future of his company; the loss of the Nippon order—more than $430 million in total revenues—would mean the forfeiture of sales momentum, the slowdown of design projects, and the discharge of production workers. He decided, and let us credit him with considerable worry and concern in that decision, to make the pledges and pay the bribes.

It is certainly easy for everyone now to condemn the decision by Mr. Kotchian to pay $3.8 million to government officials in Japan. It is much harder for most people to say that, faced with the same conditions of personal isolation, factual uncertainty, and corporate responsibility, they would not have reached the same decision. The presence of the mixed outcomes—political payoffs in Tokyo resulted in full employment in Burbank, California—and the career implications—Mr. Kotchian did not mention the possibility in his account, but it certainly has to be recognized that he would probably have been replaced as president had Lockheed lost the fourth foreign order in a row—in this instance complicate the ethical dilemma. If blame is to be ascribed—and it has to be, in this instance, for here the bribery payments were blatant, dishonest, and large—then members of the corporate staff should bear at least part of the responsibility, for they had failed to advise Mr. Kotchian of the likelihood of payoff demands so that other alternatives could be considered in advance. It is hard to think of options when demands for very substantial amounts of money are presented in a matter-of-fact manner by high government officials, with the obvious endorsement and approval of the agents for your own firm.

I have tried to describe the bribe payment by Lockheed in a reasonably sympathetic light, giving some of the extenuating circumstances, but as I stated previously, I assume that most of us agree that the payment was wrong. Why do we feel that way? Let us work through the multiple forms of analysis and see if we can substantiate our feelings.

Economically, the order was large, at $430 million. We doubtless could compute the potential profit based upon published income and expense data for prior years, but that does not seem necessary; we recognize that the order would have resulted in a substantial profit. Legally, the bribe was not unlawful; this payment was one of those acts that led to the passage of the Foreign Corrupt Practices Act, but at the time Mr. Kotchian faced the decision, payments to foreign nationals were not contrary to U.S. law. In utilitarian terms—greatest good for the greatest number—we can partially excuse the payment: The benefits of employment in Burbank are very immediate and very obvious, while the damages to the democratic process in Japan are not as obvious and quite diffused. It is in universalistic terms—everyone faced with the same set of circumstances must act in the same way—that we find definite support for our intuitive beliefs. Could we ever propose a rule that every president of a large company, faced with the potential loss of a critical order, should offer to pay 0.8 percent of the face value of that order as a bribe? In terms of justice—each act must benefit in some way the least advantaged among us—we definitely benefit only the most wealthy citizens of Japan. In terms of liberty—each act must help others to select their own course of action—we definitely restrict the ability of Japanese citizens to choose freely for themselves. I think that this multiple form of analysis leads us strictly to agree: The payment was "wrong".

ETHICAL ANALYSIS AND A JUSTIFIABLE BRIBERY CASE

Now, let us look at a bribe that I think most of us can say was certainly "permissible" if not absolutely "right". This example may be apocryphal, but it is another story that, if not true, should be. I have been told that after the passage of the Foreign Corrupt Practices Act in 1977, the board of directors of a large engineering and construction firm, with worldwide operations, decided that they would not only obey the law, they would enforce it. They set a limit of $50 that could be paid for minor services received, such as customs clearance or vehicle registration, in countries where it was customary to make those payments and where the salaries of the officials were low enough to indicate a general knowledge and acceptance of those payments. Higher payments for services were forbidden, and all payments for contract approval or sales assistance were banned. To convey this message, a group of senior executives was selected to visit each of the construction sites and supply depots. These were older men with extensive field experience, and they were known and respected by the area managers, site supervisors, and job foremen. At each site or depot, the personnel were assembled, and the executives stated clearly, "You will not pay bribes above the stated limit, and those only for services where it is both customary and known. If you do make payments, either directly or indirectly, for amounts above $50, you will be discharged, despite your length of service, with no corporate sympathy, no retirement benefits, and no severance pay. We are going to run this company the way it should be run, with high quality work and absolute financial integrity. If that is not enough, and if we can't obtain engineering and construction contracts based upon that combination, we will close the company."

The message was heard, probably with mixed reactions but doubtless with complete clarity, by the personnel at all but a few of the overseas locations. These locations were not visited because the senior executives discontinued their mission prematurely. Coming back from a remote site in the tropics, the pilot of the local airline taxied to the end of the runway, parked under the broiling sun, turned off the motors and air conditioning, and announced that he would take off after he had received a gift of

$1,200 for his daughter's wedding. The money was paid, but the executives returned to New York, for they felt that they could no longer support an authoritative policy on corrupt practices, which they had been unable to obey.

My opinion is that it is unfortunate that they discontinued their mission, for this is the most justifiable instance of bribery I know. I assume that most of you would agree. Why do we feel this way, and how can we rationalize our beliefs? Economically, the impact of the payment upon the performance of the firm was minimal, so we can disregard that form of analysis. Legally, we will have to admit that the payment was unlawful, for this event occurred after the passage of the Foreign Corrupt Practices Act. However, we saw in the chapter on the rule of law that legal requirements often do not represent moral standards, and that seems to me to be the case here. From the utilitarian point of view, I would think that the greatest good for the greatest number would come from the bribe payment, for otherwise the senior executives faced extreme discomfort and eventual illness in the stifling metal cabin of a grounded airplane, and the cost was minimal to others. From the universalist point of view, I should hope that we could agree that everyone condemned to this situation should be free to make the payment. The bribe does not decrease any opportunities for social cooperation, and it does increase the executives' ability to choose freely for themselves in the future, after their release from the plane. I am not saying that I think that the extortion of the bribe by the aircraft pilot was in any way defensible, but I do believe that the payment of the bribe by the executives of the construction company was the "right" thing to do, given the situation.

MULTIPLE ANALYSIS AND ETHICAL DILEMMAS

Multiple analysis is a useful means of rationalizing our intuitive beliefs, of justifying our almost automatic reactions, when looking at simple and obvious ethical issues such as foreign bribery. Is it, however, a useful means of reaching a decision when we truly face an ethical dilemma, when the economic and the social performance of our organization truly do seem to conflict? Will it help us decide how much we owe to our employees, customers, suppliers, distributors, stockholders, and the general public? I think that it does, and here I should like to use the ethical problems encountered by former students—the ones that were described in the first chapter, on the nature of ethics in management—as illustrations. I don't believe that in these examples it will be possible to assume agreement between us—we all have our own moral standards, based upon our different ethical systems of belief—so I will not state my conclusions, just my methods of analysis.

Pricing of Checking Account Services

Small checking accounts were determined to be unprofitable for the bank, and consequently it was felt that a charge of $5 per month and 10 cents per transaction was warranted. The ethical problem was that the bank was in an urban area with numerous older customers, many of them retired and living on Social Security, and the proposed charges would definitely diminish their standard of living.

How can this situation be analyzed? Let us start by considering alternatives. Is it possible to design a new type of checking account, perhaps limited to a set number of transactions per month, that would be less expensive to administer? Is it possible to completely automate the processing of transactions (checks and deposits) to further reduce the costs? Assuming that neither is possible, then let us move along to economic analysis. What are the costs of maintaining the small accounts used by older people? How much would those costs increase if the bank were the only one in the area not to make a monthly or transaction charge to retired customers, and consequently almost all of those people moved their accounts to this bank? What would the revenues be if the charges were instituted? How many customers would close their accounts, even though they are naturally afraid to carry cash, and reduce both our income and our expenses?

Legal analysis is next. There is certainly no law against charging a fee for financial services, yet the bank can doubtless expect some protest by social and political organizations in the area that would voice an objection to charging a fee that falls primarily on low-income, retired persons. The fee would contravene the presumed moral standards of a considerable segment of the population and might eventually lead to legal restrictions.

Finally, let us think about moral analysis. Universalism—everyone faced with a given situation should be forced to take the same action or make the same decision—does not seem too relevant here; I would be willing to have every banker faced with unprofitable accounts charge a fee for those accounts, were it not for the unfortunate consequences of that action in this instance. Utilitarianism, which deals with the consequences, *is* relevant here; it is often translated as "the greatest good for the greatest number," but those two combined concepts don't really help in moral analysis because it is hard to measure the greatest good or identify the greatest number. It is more useful in analyzing ethical dilemmas to think of utilitarianism as cost/benefit analysis, with the added step of considering who receives the benefits and who bears the costs. The benefits will go to the wealthier members of the community, as they are the large depositors who will receive the interest payments, or they are the stockholders of the bank, who will receive the dividends, while the costs will be borne by the older and poorer people in the area. That is troublesome. It certainly goes against the dictum of Professor Rawls that inequality in the distribution of benefits is legitimate, provided it in some way helps the less advantaged members of society. It also goes against the dictum of Professor Nozick that actions should increase, not decrease, the ability of members of society to make their own decisions and lead their own lives.

How would I decide? I'm not certain—and I said earlier that I would not impose my views upon you—but at least I feel that I understand this situation much more fully and would be better able to explain my decision to others and support it rationally.

Exaggerated or Misleading Claims in Advertising

The ethical problem in this instance centered on advertising statements that were intended to deceive. "Up 387 percent over the past three years" was the heading on a mutual fund ad; it was accurate only over that specific time period—over a longer time span the fund had not kept pace with the growth in the Dow Jones averages. "8½ percent interest" was the heading on a money market fund; there was a small asterisk, and down at the bottom of the page a footnote that explained that the interest rate was for the first month only. "Insured by [name of an insurance company]" was stated on every advertisement that mentioned customer accounts; the ads did not explain that the insurance company—which had an impressively fictitious name, such as Travelers Equitable of Wausau—was a wholly owned and poorly financed subsidiary.

How do we analyze this situation? Start once again by looking at alternatives. Is it possible to develop an ad campaign that will be both more effective and more truthful? I think that we can assume that the client—a financial services firm—was not irrevocably committed to being untruthful; they just wanted an advertising program that increased their number of customers and believed that deceptive statements would accomplish that purpose.

If the client does not wish to change the approach, then it is necessary to look at the economics of the ad campaign. What is the probable increase in revenues that can be directly attributed to the deceptive advertising, and how do these marginal revenues compare to the media costs? Most of us would like to believe that misleading slogans are not effective; that potential customers quickly see through that sort of untruth. Perhaps, however, we will find from market research that the ads are effective. They clearly are not illegal—or we would not see so many that are similar in some sense—so we have to move to ethical analysis and moral reasoning.

Universalism seems to be most useful here, for the utilitarian distribution of benefits and costs from deceptive advertising does not seem to be inherently unjust, and customers do have some obligation to be wary of untrue claims. The primary question of universalism is "Are you willing to agree that every advertiser, wishing to increase revenues, should be free to make deliberately deceptive statements?" Let me explain, once again, that in using this first formulation of the Categorical Imperative it is important not to think of the consequences of the act, for that would bring in utilitarian concepts related to outcomes, and you would then not be building your ethical system of belief on a single principle. In this case, the single principle is your duty to other people to be consistent. You must think about the type of world you want: If you want a world in which judges don't try to deceive you, doctors don't try to deceive you, teachers don't try to deceive you, and friends don't try to deceive you, then you must be consistent and agree that advertisers should not try to do so either.

You could also look at the second formulation of the Categorical Imperative, which states that it is necessary to treat other people as ends in themselves, not as means to our ends. This means that we should consider other people to be individuals worthy of dignity and respect, pursuing their own goals of happiness and self-improvement. The deliberate misleading of others does not seem to be treating them with dignity and respect; instead, it seems to be treating them solely as means to the goal of the deceptive advertiser.

Misuse of Frequent Flyer Discounts and Trips

Most frequent flyers travel on business. There is the ethical question of the propriety of giving the bonuses, which in essence are rebates on the price of the ticket, to the traveler and not to the company paying for the travel. The marketing reasons for doing so are clear: It is the traveler who decides which airline he or she will take. One can certainly look at this issue from an economic view; business travelers should be representing the owners of the company, and they are not exercising their responsibilities toward those owners by accepting the price rebates themselves instead of passing those rebates along to the stockholders. The utilitarian view is also relevant; the benefits go to the individual, while the costs are assigned to the company and to the nonbusiness travelers who normally do not fly frequently enough to accumulate enough discounts to qualify for a free trip. But, neither view seems particularly compelling. Any company could insist that the rebates be returned to the firm, to reduce executive travel costs, and nonbusiness travelers are only being penalized because they don't travel enough to generate economies of scale in providing the service. Apparent inequities in the distribution of benefits or the allocation of costs that can be justified economically through the economies of scale or scope or the integration of operations are not truly inequitable.

The more interesting issue in this instance is not the ethical problem of the price rebates, but the managerial actions of the executive who insisted that others in his department accumulate their credits for his use. This is not an ethical dilemma in the true sense of the term, for clearly there is no conflict between the economic performance and the social performance of the firm. This is an ethical problem only in that it represents personal dishonesty; it is theft taking some property or benefit that belongs to others for an individual's own use. There may be no way the former student who explained this situation to me can prevent her superior from doing this to others—given that apparently the chairman of the firm either approved or would approve of the practice if he knew of it—but she can certainly prevent him from forcing her to participate. It would be very difficult for her superior to adversely affect her career for refusing to participate, for he could not accuse her of a lack of cooperation without accusing himself of theft.

Working Conditions in a Manufacturing Plant

"The noise, the heat, the fumes, and the pace of work are close to intolerable" was the statement made to me, yet it was explained that funds would not be allocated to improve conditions without showing a substantial internal rate of return. Here it would seem that economic analysis would be most meaningful. What are the costs in plant downtime, worker absence, and employee illness that bring low productivity and poor quality? How much could output and quality be improved, given better conditions? Economic theory insists that all costs be computed, including the personal costs of job safety and the social costs of environmental pollution; when this is done, remedial actions often do become economically rational.

Let us assume that this is an instance where improvements in the working conditions cannot be economically justified. Let us also assume that these working conditions are marginally lawful. What do we do then? Obviously, we are forced to use moral analysis, but moral analysis looking at alternatives, not just condemning the existing situation. Utilitarianism seems useful here. Who receives the benefits and who bears the costs of closing the plant? If we reduce the work force or decrease the pay scale in order to make the improvements economically justifiable, then who receives what benefits, and who bears what costs? It is difficult to conceive of viable alternatives in depressed basic industries such as steel stampings and iron foundries, but it is important in moral analysis to go beyond simple yes-or-no choices. Professor Rawls's concept of social cooperation and distributive justice also seems relevant in looking at this situation: Which of these alternatives would most benefit the least advantaged among the members of the organization, who doubtless were the hourly paid employees?

Customer Service and Declining Product Quality

The issue here was warranty repairs on new automobiles and the hesitancy of both dealers and company representatives to authorize major work due to budget limitations. In the last illustration, we saw the necessity to look at multiple alternatives in ethical analysis; in this instance, there is a need to consider the extended consequences. The extended consequences of customer dissatisfaction with the product quality of American cars has been expressed as a growing market share for Japanese imports. That is not totally an accurate statement; other factors than a reputation for better product quality—among them lower wage rates and a favorable foreign exchange—have also been responsible for the trend toward foreign cars. But, the economic results of such issues as poor product quality and adverse working conditions are a valid input in moral reasoning.

Extended consequences—the expected outcomes spread throughout society over the long term—are obviously important in ethical analysis. Some people have even claimed that an ethical approach to management is only the consideration of the long term rather than the short term and the recognition of the dispersed rather than the focused effects of a decision or action. This would appear to be an exaggeration, for it provides no means of analyzing those effects, but it does indicate the importance of looking beyond the immediate, concentrated outcomes.

Economic analysis would indicate generally a need for improved customer service in the automobile industry. Legal analysis would show certainly a widespread public insistence upon improved service, leading to the passage of "lemon laws" in many states. Moral analysis through utilitarianism would seem to add little understanding; the benefits accruing to the customer would be exactly balanced by the costs allocated to the company, and it is hard to think of new-car buyers as the "greatest number" deserving of any "greatest good" in our society. Universalism and the two formulations of the Categorical Imperative are much more useful in this instance. Would we be willing to have every manufacturer of a defective product, when faced with a demand for repair or replacement, delay or attempt halfway measures? When we do delay or attempt halfway measures, are we treating our customers as ends in themselves, worthy of dignity and respect, or are we treating them as means to our own ends? The answer here would seem to be clear.

Work-Force Reductions

This is a difficult issue because the economic returns and the social obligations of the company are so directly in conflict. It is necessary to look at the alternatives, but many of these alternatives are weak. Early retirement has a nice "voluntary" sound, but it is alleged not to be truly voluntary in some instances; and outplacement may be just a synonym for "We'll help you write your resume." The true problem may be that, given the competitive nature of many basic industries, the number of alternatives for meaningful cost reduction is limited.

Economic analysis is useful here. Exactly what will be the financial consequences of creating a smaller organization? Obviously, the overhead will be reduced, but will the competitive capability—in product development, market expansion, customer service, quality control, and worker productivity—improve? It is necessary for us to admit that some organizations have become so large, with so many layers of middle managers and so many groups of staff between the senior executives who can allocate resources and the operating personnel who can use them, that it is hard to improve competitive performance without middle management cutbacks. But, it is also necessary to admit that many work-force reductions impede rather than improve product development, market expansion, and so forth.

Moral analysis in work-force reductions has to focus on utilitarianism: Who receives the benefits and who bears the costs, and is there any acceptable way to lessen those costs or to redistribute those benefits? Here, high managerial salaries seem to be relevant; would it be more equitable to spend more on the retraining and assistance of displaced workers and less on the salaries and bonuses of senior executives? This is an issue that will be faced by many persons concerned with an ethical approach to management as business conditions become more global and more competitive, and as managerial salaries and bonuses become much higher and less market driven.

Environmental Pollution

Pollution is a major problem faced by our society, with obvious consequences for individual health, recreational opportunities, and the quality of life for all. Why does improper disposal of chemical wastes continue? Probably it continues partially because of the uncertainty associated with improper disposal; it is hard for many people to realize that 5 gallons, or even 50 gallons, of a chemical used routinely in industry will be all that harmful when dumped in a landfill or a stream. And in many instances they are correct: 5 gallons or even 50 gallons is not that harmful by itself; it is the aggregate of many 5 and 50 gallon amounts over a lengthy period of time that becomes exceedingly harmful.

In the illustration cited in the first chapter, a former student found that industrial solvents and degreasing solutions were being poured down a storm drain. I understand that, unfortunately, this is a common method of disposal. Economic analysis would reveal that the cost of proper disposal is often very high, which leads towards improper disposal. Legal analysis would show that this improper disposal is certainly unlawful, but the law is difficult to enforce because of the problems of tracing the sources of pollution, whether the materials are poured into a public sewer or dumped on a vacant lot. Moral analysis, however, would seem to be very definite. The greatest good for the greatest number obviously would indicate the need for proper combustion or burial, and few people would agree that all other firms needing to dispose of used chemical compounds should be free to just dump the material, secretly, into sewers or onto the landscape.

Property Tax Reductions

A major employer within a local community has substantial economic power, particularly if the employer has multiple plants in other locations and consequently can move production and employment between the plants. This economic power is often used in pressing for tax concessions. In the illustration given in the first chapter, a company was pressing for a 50 percent tax reduction, two years after they had received a 24 percent reduction. A large reduction of this nature would obviously impose tax increases or service reductions on the residents of the community.

Economic analysis would attempt to balance the benefits received by the community from the manufacturing plant, in the form of employment and tax payments, with the costs imposed on the community for the services needed by the plant and by the employees. But the balance of benefits and costs is not truly relevant in this instance. Here, we have to be concerned with the equitable receipt of those benefits and equitable allocation of those costs, and this requires the Utilitarian form of moral analysis. If we can establish, through legal analysis, that the tax assessment procedures were properly followed by the community and that the tax rates are approximately equal for all classes or types of property, then the question we face is whether it is "proper" or "right" or "just" for residents who are not employed by the plant, and consequently receive none of the benefits, to be forced to pay part of the costs. I promised not to state my opinions on these ethical issues, but in this instance I will break that promise: The use of economic power to impose economic penalties on others seems to me to be totally wrong.

MULTIPLE ANALYSIS AND "DRAWING THE LINE"

Ethical decisions of the nature that have been described above are not simple choices between right and wrong; they are complex judgments on the balance between the economic performance and the social performance of the organization. In all of the nine instances that were discussed—except for the personal dishonesty in the instance of the airline ticket rebates—the economic performance of the firm—measured by sales revenues, variable costs, fixed expenses, or net profits—would be improved. In all of the nine cases that were discussed, the social performance of the firm—much more difficult to measure but expressed as some form of obligation to the managers, workers, customers, suppliers, distributors and members of the local community—would be reduced. The question, in each, became, in summary, "What do we owe to our managers, our workers, our customers, our suppliers, our distributors, and our community?" How do we balance economic performance and social performance?

These are difficult questions to answer. They are difficult because of the essential conflict between the two dissimilar quantities: economic performance and social performance. They are also difficult because each question has numerous alternative solutions—these are not simple yes-or-no choices—and the consequences of the alternatives extend throughout society, with outcomes in which the benefits and costs are often mixed, and the probabilities of those outcomes are frequently uncertain. How do we decide when faced with ethical problems of this complexity? Multiple analysis—using economic, legal and moral forms of reasoning—appears to me to make the issues much clearer and to make the "right" or "proper" or "just" decision more readily apparent.

Unfortunately, reaching the "right" or "proper" or "just" answer often is not enough. It is also necessary to decide when you will insist that your view of what is "right" and "proper" and "just" be recognized and then implemented by the organization. It is often possible to explain your thinking to people and to gain some converts. It is even possible to demonstrate your analysis to others and gain some more. But it is seldom possible to achieve unanimity in an ethical dilemma, because each individual's moral standards are so personal, and so deeply held. Managers will often compromise on marketing, production, and financial problems; they generally will not compromise on major ethical issues.

What do you do when you feel strongly about an ethical problem—a conflict between the economic performance and the social performance of your firm—and you find that no compromise is possible? Do you walk away from the problem, or do you take some action? Where do you draw the line?

First, it is necessary to recognize that people can legitimately differ in their views of what should be done to resolve an ethical dilemma. A refusal to compromise does not automatically mean that others in the organization are wrong. People can differ on ethical issues because the relative weighting they place on the economic, legal, and moral forms of analysis may vary. People may differ because the ethical systems upon which their standards for moral reasoning are based can vary. And, it is also necessary to recognize that people can differ in their views of what constitutes an ethical dilemma. Some people are much less concerned with social performance and much more concerned with economic performance than others. What do you do under those circumstances, if you find a situation or an issue you believe to be deeply wrong according to your personal moral standards, yet you recognize that you are in the minority within your portion of the organization?

Let us assume that you are not the president or a senior executive of your company, able to take whatever action you believe to be just. Let us also assume that the firm has no ombudsman—generally an older and respected member of the organization who has been relieved of direct responsibility for management and has been designated to counsel privately with other employees on personal problems and ethical issues. Let us finally assume that you have looked for alternatives and found none, and that you have tried to explain your concerns to your immediate superior and have been rejected. What do you do? What do you do if you have found large amounts of toxic wastes being stored in leaking 55-gallon drums and have been told, "Forget it; it's none of your business"? What do you do if you have found that employees are being subjected to unsafe working conditions and have been told, "We don't have the money to fix it"? What do you do if you find that payments are being made to some purchasing agents to influence their decisions and have been told, "Keep quiet about this; it goes on all the time"? Where do you draw the line between what you will accept and what you will not accept?

This is the most fundamental moral issue in management, for it places a person's career in jeopardy. How do you decide if the resolution of the ethical dilemma you have encountered is worth your career? I think that it necessary to use only the most basic moral reasoning:

1. *Beneficiency.* Who is going to be hurt, and how badly?

2. *Consistency.* Could I permit everyone to take this same action?

3. *Justice.* Will the least advantaged among us be treated the worst?

4. *Liberty.* Will this reduce the opportunities of any individuals or groups for free, informed choice?

In the next chapter we will look at changes in the structure and systems of an organization that can more readily resolve the ethical conflicts between economic and social performance, and more easily avoid the necessity for an individual to make the fundamental moral choice between his or her career and his or her responsibility.

CASES

George Kacmarek

George Kacmarek was a graduate of the BBA program at the University of Michigan. He went to work for one of the large auto supply firms in Detroit that produced stamped metal parts for the car companies. The following is an almost verbatim account of a moral problem he encountered during his first week on the job.

> On the second or third day at work, I was sent from the office out to the plant to pick up some requisition slips from the foreman in one of the tool rooms. I don't know if you have ever been in a big stamping plant, but they are noisy and confusing. They have these big presses going up and coming down, and you can't hear yourself think. In our plant they have more than 100 presses, all under one roof, but with paint booths, tool cribs, loading docks, and storage bins scattered all around. I got lost.
>
> I didn't want to admit that I was lost, so I couldn't ask any of the workers for directions. They probably couldn't hear me anyway. I went into what I thought would be an office where I could ask for directions, but it was a record storage area, with row after row of steel shelving reaching close to the ceiling, loaded with thousands of cardboard files, each marked by a number. There was a door at one end, and I was heading in that direction when I heard the voice of the plant manager talking to another person. The plant manager was from New York City and had an accent that you could remember very easily. I had only met him once, but I recognized his voice right away.

The plant manager said, "I want $5,000 this time. That's a nice round figure, and it will help me to remember [name of a large steel supply firm] for the rest of the year."

The other person said, "George, you're getting greedy. You've given us good business, and we appreciate it, but its not worth five bills."

The plant manager got upset and told the man, "Look, you'll be out on your fat rear end if I say the word. We'll start running quality checks on your stuff until we find some that won't meet specs, and then we'll reject everything you've sent us for a month."

This didn't faze the other guy at all; he said, "George, we know the score. You don't have to tell us. But we can't go $5,000. We'll go $3,000 now, and $3,000 at the end of the year if everything stays smooth and if your volume holds up, but that's the best that we can do."

The plant manager grumbled about that, but eventually he agreed to it, and both men went out the door at the end without seeing me. I went out the other door as fast as I could and wandered around on the shop floor for a while. I didn't know what to do.

Class Assignment. What would you do in this situation? Make a set of specific recommendations for George Kacmarek.

Sarah Goodwin

Sarah Goodwin was a graduate of an MBA program on the West Coast. She had majored in marketing, was interested in retailing, and had been delighted to receive a job offer from a large and prestigious department store chain in northern California. The first year of employment at this chain was considered to be a training program, but formal instruction was very limited. Instead, after a quick tour of the facilities and a welcoming speech by the president, each of the new trainees was assigned to work as an assistant to a buyer in one of the departments. The intent was that the trainees would work with five or six buyers during the year, rotating assignments every two months, and would make themselves useful enough during those assignments so that at least one buyer would ask to have that person join his or her department on a permanent basis.

Buyers are critical in the management of a department store. They select the goods to be offered, negotiate purchase terms, set retail prices, arrange displays, and organize promotions; they are generally responsible for the operations of the departments within the store. Each buyer acts as a profit center, and sales figures and profit margins are reported monthly to the senior executives. In this particular chain, the sales and profits were calculated on a square-foot basis (that is, per square foot of floor space occupied by the department), and the buyers contended, generally on a friendly basis, to outperform each other so that their square footage would be expanded. The buyers received substantial commissions based upon monthly profits.

Sarah's first assignment was to work for the buyer of the gourmet food department. This was a small unit at the main store that sold packaged food items such as jams and jellies, crackers and cookies, cheese and spreads, and candies, most of which were imported from Europe. The department also offered preserved foods, such as smoked fish and meats, and some expensive delicacies such as caviar, truffles, and estate-bottled wines. Many of the items were packaged as gifts, in boxes or baskets, with decorative wrapping and ties.

Sarah was originally disappointed to have been sent to such a small and specialized department rather than to a larger one that dealt with more general fashion goods, but she soon found that this assignment was considered to be a plum. The buyer, Maria Castellani, was a well-known personality throughout the store; witty, competent, and sarcastic, she served as a sounding board, consultant, and friend to the other buyers. She would evaluate fashions, forecast trends, chastise managers (managers in a department store are the people associated with finance, personnel, accounting, or planning, not merchandising), and discuss retailing events and changes in an amusing, informative way. Everybody in the store seemed to find a reason to stop by the gourmet food department at least once during each day to chat with Maria. Sarah was naturally included in these conversations, and consequently she found that she was getting to know all of the other buyers and could ask one of them to request her as an assistant at the next rotation of assignments.

For the first five weeks of her employment, Sarah was exceptionally happy, pleased with her career and her life. She was living in a house on one of the cable car lines, with three other professionally employed women. She felt that she was performing well on her first job and making sensible arrangements for her next assignment. Then, an event occurred that threatened to destroy all of her contentment:

> We had received a shipment of thin little wafers from England that had a creme filling flavored with fruit: strawberries and raspberries. They were very good. They were packaged in foil-covered boxes, but somehow they had become infested with insects.
>
> We did not think that all of the boxes were infested, because not all of the customers brought them back. But some people did, and obviously we could not continue to sell them. We couldn't inspect the packages and keep the ones that were not infested, because there were too many—about $9,000 worth—and because we would have to tear the foil to open each box. Maria said that the manufacturer would not give us a refund because the infestation doubtless occurred during shipment or even during storage at our own warehouse.
>
> Maria told me to get rid of them. I thought that she meant for me to arrange to have them taken to the dump, but she said, "Absolutely not. Call [name of an executive] at [name of a convenience store chain in southern California]. They operate down in the ghetto and can sell anything. We've got to get our money back."

Class Assignment. What would you do in this situation? Make a set of specific recommendations for Sarah Goodwin.

Roger Worsham

Roger Worsham was a 32-year-old graduate of the MBA program at the University of Michigan. He had majored in accounting but had found it difficult to get a job offer during his second year in the program. He had interviewed with all six of the large national CPA firms and had been rejected by all of them. He had also interviewed with a number of medium-size regional firms that came to the university recruiting employees but had been rejected there also.

The director of placement at the School of Business Administration told Roger that the problem was his age; she said that accounting firms were exceedingly hesitant to hire anyone over 28 to 30 years old because they felt that older entrants were unlikely to stay with the firm over the first few years of auditing, which some people found to be dull and tedious. Roger, however, felt that perhaps his personality was more at fault than his age. He found it difficult to converse easily in the interviews, and he was afraid that he projected himself as a hesitant, uncertain individual. After graduating from college, he had worked for seven years as a teacher in a primary school, and interviewers always asked about his decision to change careers, seeming to imply that he was not certain about his objectives in life or his commitment to accounting.

At the suggestion of the faculty member who taught the small business management course at the university, Roger applied to some of the small, local CPA firms in the state. He was accepted almost immediately by Arnold Abramson and Company.

Arnold Abramson and Company was a small accounting firm that served a large geographic area with a limited industrial base in northern Michigan and Wisconsin. The firm had been founded in 1946 in Bay City, Michigan (approximately 100 miles north of Detroit) when Mr. Abramson returned from army service after the Second World War. Helped by the economic growth of the postwar period, his company expanded rapidly, and by 1960 it had offices in Flint and Detroit to the south, and in Traverse City, Petosky, and Alpena to the north. Eventually the firm spread across the Upper Peninsula of Michigan and into the northern counties of Wisconsin.

The southern offices of Abramson and Company, in Flint and Detroit, competed directly with the large, national CPA firms, the so-called (at that time) Big Eight, but they were able to operate successfully until the mid-1970s by providing more personalized services and by charging somewhat lower rates. However, competition increased sharply in the late 1970s and early 1980s as the tax laws became more complex, the auditing procedures more exact, and the bookkeeping more automated. The Big Eight firms were able, through their extensive training programs and their continual staff additions, to provide greater help and assistance to their clients on tax returns and computer systems, and many of the companies that had been clients of Arnold Abramson and Company for years switched to one of the national firms. It was eventually necessary to close the Flint and Detroit offices.

Some of the partners of Arnold Abramson and Company recommended the merger of their company with one of the national CPA firms, but the founder, Arnold Abramson, was not only still living but still active, and he and his two sons were steadfast in their opposition to any sale or merger. They believed that their past policies of personal attention, prompt response, and reduced cost would maintain the firm in the smaller cities and towns of northern Michigan and Wisconsin. Even when some of their clients in those areas felt it was necessary to obtain the data-processing assistance and tax expertise of the national firms, Mr. Abramson and his two sons continued to resist any possibility of merger and continued to stress their strategy of personalized service at lower cost. Roger Worsham summarized his impression of this "We won't quit" attitude very vividly to the case writer:

> The old gentleman was 84 when I joined the firm, and he simply was not going to surrender to Arthur Andersen or Price Waterhouse. And, you know, he had a point: There is room left in the world for the more personal approach, even in auditing. The old man was adamant about this. I understand that at the partners' dinner this year he laid it right on the line to the other members of the firm. "You are to keep the local banks, retail stores, and small manufacturers as your clients; if you lose your clients to those people from Detroit, we'll shut down your office." He always referred to representatives of the Big Eight firms as "those people from Detroit" even though they might be from offices in Lansing, Grand Rapids, or Milwaukee.

Roger Worsham was assigned to one of the northern offices, and he moved his family (wife and two small children) to the area and started work immediately after graduation. In the first six months, he participated in the audit of a savings and loan association, a farm equipment dealership, a large retail hardware store, and a nearly bankrupt machinery manufacturing firm. His family enjoyed the area in which they were living, he enjoyed the work that he was doing, and he felt that his life was beginning to take on direction and purpose. But then he found clear evidence of fraud and encountered a situation that threatened his newly found security and employment.

We were finishing the annual audit for the machinery manufacturer. This company had not been doing well; sales had been declining for four or five years, losses had been reported for each of those years, and the financial position of the company had steadily deteriorated. I was going through the notes payable and found that they had a loan, and a large one, from the savings and loan association.

Now, first, it is illegal for a savings and loan association in Michigan to make a loan to a manufacturing company. It is against state law. But, even more, I knew that this loan was not on the books of the savings and loan since I had been the one to audit the loan portfolio there. I had looked at every loan in the file—I had not statistically sampled from the file, which is the way you would usually do it—and had checked each loan to see that it was supported by a properly assigned mortgage and a currently valid appraisal. The only thing I had not done was to add up the total for the file to check with the reported total, since the usual way is to sample, and you don't get a total when you sample. I still had my working papers back at our office, of course, so I went back and ran the total and, sure enough, it was off by the amount of the loan to the manufacturing company.

It was obvious what had happened: Someone had taken the folder cover of the illegal loan out of the file prior to our audit at the savings and loan. It became obvious who had done it: The president of the savings and loan was a lawyer in the town who, I found by checking the stockholder lists, was the largest owner of the manufacturing company. He was also on the board of directors of the local bank and reputedly was a wealthy, powerful person in the community.

I took my working papers and a Xerox copy of the ledger showing the loan and went to see the partner in charge of our office the next morning. He listened to me without saying a word, and when I finished he told me, "I will take care of this privately. We simply cannot afford to lose a client of the status of [name of the lawyer]. You put the papers you have through the shredder."

I was astonished. The AICPA code of ethics and the generally accepted auditing standards both require that you either resign from the engagement or issue an adverse opinion when you find irregularities. This was not a small amount. The loan was not only illegal, it was in default, and would adversely affect the savings and loan association.

I hesitated, because I was surprised and shocked, and he told me, "I will not tell you again. You put those papers through the shredder or I'll guarantee that you'll never get a CPA in Michigan, or work in an accounting office in this state for the rest of your life."

I didn't know what to do.

Class Assignment. What would you do in this situation? Make a set of specific recommendations for Roger Worsham.

CHAPTER 6

Managerial Ethics and Organizational Design

We are concerned in this book with ethical dilemmas: decisions and actions faced by managers in which the economic performance and the social performance of the organization are in conflict. These are situations in which someone to whom the organization has some form of obligation—employees, customers, suppliers, distributors, stockholders, or the general population in the area where the company operates—is going to be hurt or harmed in some way, while the company is going to profit. The question is how to decide: how to find a balance between economic performance and social performance that a manager can say with some degree of certainty is "right" and "proper" and "just".

In the last chapter, it was suggested that it is necessary for a manager facing an ethical dilemma to use multiple forms of analysis—to make use of economic concepts, legal precepts, and philosophical principles in sequence to find that balance. After all, if a manager's decision or action follows impersonal market forces, conforms to published legal requirements, provides substantial benefits to large numbers of people, is an action we can wish that everyone would take when faced with the same set of decision alternatives and background factors, is "fair" in the sense of increasing the willingness of others to work toward greater social cooperation, and is "open" in the sense of expanding the ability of others to choose for themselves, then perhaps we can say with some degree of certainty that that decision is "right" and "proper" and "just".

So far, however, we have thought of the managers facing these ethical dilemmas in which the social performance and the economic performance of their firms are in obvious conflict as being free individuals, isolated from organizational influences, able to choose the "right" and "proper" and "just" as they see the "right" and "proper" and "just". That may not be an accurate view. There may be explicit organizational pressures that affect that choice. These organizational pressures may tend to push the decision away from the social performance and toward the economic performance of the firm. These organizational pressures may be so extreme that they force the manager to make the fundamental moral choice between his or her personal career and his or her social responsibility.

Let us look at some of these fundamental moral choices and explicit organizational pressures, and let us use as an example one of the most damaging industrial accidents of the past decade: the wreck of the *Exxon Valdez*.

THE WRECK OF THE *EXXON VALDEZ*

At 9:30 P.M. on Thursday, March 22, 1990, the oil tanker *Exxon Valdez* left the oil terminal at Valdez, Alaska, loaded with 1.26 million barrels of crude petroleum from the North Slope producing fields. The *Valdez* is the largest tanker owned by Exxon. It is nearly 1,000 feet long and weighs, fully loaded, 280,000 tons.

When the ship left port, it was under the command of Captain William Murphy, the harbor pilot. Harbor pilots are responsible for steering both incoming and outgoing tankers through the Valdez Narrows, a half-mile-wide approach to the port at Valdez. After exiting the Valdez Narrows and achieving the sea-lanes in Prince William Sound, Captain Murphy turned over command to Captain Joseph Hazelwood and left the ship. (See Exhibit 6–1 for a graphic display of the hour before the wreck.) Captain Murphy testified later that he had smelled alcohol on the breath of Captain Hazelwood, but that he had made no comment and had taken no action. He knew that it was common practice for both the officers and crew of oil tankers to drink while in port.

Captain Hazelwood, immediately after assuming command, radioed the Coast Guard and requested permission to alter course

EXHIBIT 6–1

Diagram of the Approaches to Valdez Harbor, and Listing of the Events that Led to the Accident on March 24, 1989

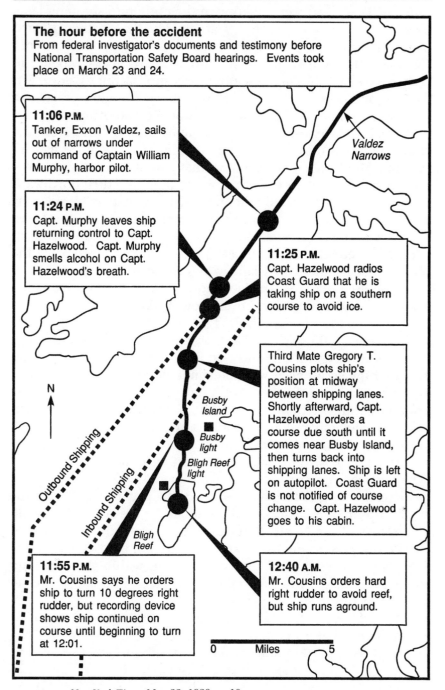

The hour before the accident
From federal investigator's documents and testimony before National Transportation Safety Board hearings. Events took place on March 23 and 24.

Valdez Narrows

11:06 P.M.
Tanker, Exxon Valdez, sails out of narrows under command of Captain William Murphy, harbor pilot.

11:24 P.M.
Capt. Murphy leaves ship returning control to Capt. Hazelwood. Capt. Murphy smells alcohol on Capt. Hazelwood's breath.

11:25 P.M.
Capt. Hazelwood radios Coast Guard that he is taking ship on a southern course to avoid ice.

Third Mate Gregory T. Cousins plots ship's position at midway between shipping lanes. Shortly afterward, Capt. Hazelwood orders a course due south until it comes near Busby Island, then turns back into shipping lanes. Ship is left on autopilot. Coast Guard is not notified of course change. Capt. Hazelwood goes to his cabin.

N

Busby Island

Busby light

Bligh Reef light

Outbound Shipping

Inbound Shipping

Bligh Reef

11:55 P.M.
Mr. Cousins says he orders ship to turn 10 degrees right rudder, but recording device shows ship continued on course until beginning to turn at 12:01.

12:40 A.M.
Mr. Cousins orders hard right rudder to avoid reef, but ship runs aground.

0   Miles   5

SOURCE: *New York Times*, May 22, 1989, p. 10.

to avoid large chunks of ice that had broken loose from the Columbia Glacier and were floating in the outbound shipping lane. The permission was granted. Captain Hazelwood then turned over command of the vessel to the third mate, Mr. Gregory Cousins, and went below to his cabin. Mr. Cousins was not licensed to pilot a ship in the sea channels approaching Valdez. Mr. Cousins and others later testified that it was common practice to turn over command of oil tankers to nonlicensed officers.

Captain Hazelwood had set the automatic pilot to steer the ship southward into the inbound shipping lane, and he had instructed Mr. Cousins to maintain that course until after the ice chunks from the glaciers were past and then to return northward to the outbound lane. No inbound traffic was expected, and permission for this course change had been granted by the Coast Guard, so no danger was anticipated. At 11:55 P.M., Mr. Cousins ordered a course change of 10 degrees right rudder to bring the tanker back to the proper lane within the channel. There was no response. At 12:04 A.M., the lookout, who was on the bridge rather than at the normal station on the bow of the tanker, sighted the lighted buoy marking Bligh Reef, a rock outcropping only 13 to 40 feet beneath the surface. Mr. Cousins ordered emergency hard right rudder. Again, there was no response. In the hearings that followed the accident, it was determined that either Captain Hazelwood had not informed Mr. Cousins that he had placed the ship on automatic pilot, or that Mr. Cousins and the helmsman had not remembered to disconnect the automatic pilot, which prevented manual steering of the vessel.

At 12:05 A.M. the *Exxon Valdez* ran aground on Bligh Reef. The hull was punctured in numerous places. 260,000 barrels, approximately 11 million gallons of crude oil, began to spill from the badly ruptured tanks. It would eventually be the largest oil spill in the history of the North American petroleum industry. It would eventually cause immense harm, estimated in the billions of dollars, to the livelihood of the people living within the area, and immense damage, which cannot be estimated in dollar terms, to the quality of the Alaskan environment.

At 12:28 A.M., one of the officers on the ship radioed to the Coast Guard that it was aground on Bligh Reef. "Are you leaking oil?" a Coast Guard operator asked. "I think so," was the reply.[1]

At 3:23 A.M., members of the Coast Guard boarded the *Exxon Valdez* and reported that oil was gushing from the tanker. "We've got a serious problem," radioed the Coast Guard officer on board the tanker. "There's nobody here. . . . Where's Alyeska?"[2]

AFTERMATH OF THE WRECK

Alyeska is the Alyeska Pipeline Service Company, which both managed the oil pipeline that brought crude oil 800 miles from the oil fields at Prudhoe Bay to Valdez and ran the oil terminal at Valdez. It was responsible through a formal agreement with the state of Alaska for the containment and recovery of all oil spills within the harbor and sea-lanes leading toward Valdez. That agreement was expressed in a detailed written plan, 250 pages long, which listed the equipment and personnel that were to be kept available by Alyeska and the actions that were to be taken by Alyeska to react promptly to oil spills. The stated goal of the plan was to encircle any serious oil spill with floating containment booms with 5 hours of the first report of the occurrence and to recover 50 percent of the spill within 48 hours. The stated goal was well-known within the area and accounted for the perplexity of the Coast Guard officer. When he reported, "There's nobody here," he was referring not to the captain and crew of the tanker, but to the oil spill recovery team and equipment from Alyeska.

At 6:00 A.M. on Friday, March 23 (six hours after the accident), officials from Exxon flew over the grounded tanker for the first time and reported a massive oil slick streaming away from the tanker. They contacted the Alyeska oil terminal and ordered a quicker response and greater effort from the personnel at the terminal. The problem, the manager at the terminal reported, was that the single barge capable of handling the long containment booms had been out of service for nine weeks and had been unloaded for repairs. They could still use the barge, despite the lack of repair, but the single employee who was capable of operating the crane needed for reloading had not yet reported for work. When that employee was contacted (it was his day off) and did report, it was found that only about half of the containment booms that were listed in the emergency plan and should have been readily available were actually in stock. By 2:30 P.M., the barge was loaded and had departed for the wreck site, carrying all of the containment booms that were available and a number of centrifugal pumps to help in removing the remaining oil from the *Valdez*. None of the 10-inch-diameter hoses, which would be needed to connect the pumps and transfer the oil, could be found among the emergency supplies; it was necessary to fly lengths of the huge hoses from Seattle to Valdez. The transfer of the remaining oil in the *Valdez* was delayed until those hoses arrived.

At 7:36 A.M. on Saturday, March 24 (31½ hours after the accident), Exxon began pumping oil from the *Valdez* to a second tanker moored alongside, the *Baton Rouge*. At about the same time, seven Alyeska "skimmers," or boats with vacuum equipment designed to siphon oil off the surface of the water, arrived at the site. The skimmers, however, were designed to recover oil that had been bunched in a compact mass by the containment booms. Those booms were still not in place, due to a shortage of tugs and some degree of confusion in the means of unloading the heavy booms, connecting them, and placing them in the sea. By nightfall, only 1,200 barrels of oil had been recovered by the skimmers.

At 11:00 A.M. on Sunday, March 25 (59 hours after the accident), the *Exxon Valdez* was finally encircled by containment booms. It had taken two and a half days to set the booms in place, despite the original plan, which called for full containment of any spill within five hours. Because of the shortage of booms, most of the oil was outside the containment area, in a slick that now covered 12 square miles. The wave action had begun to convert the crude oil to an emulsified "mousse," a mixture of oil and water that quadrupled the volume. This emulsified mixture now lay 5 to 9 inches thick upon the surface of the sea, and winds were spreading that mixture throughout Prince William Sound. It had begun to swathe the islands and beaches with solid black bands of petroleum "gunk," the accepted term for the residue that is left after the more volatile elements in crude oil have evaporated. Eventually, the mousse mixture would stretch 700 miles along the Alaskan coastline, spoiling fishery resources, wildlife refuges, and national parks in one of the most scenic regions of the world and killing birds, fish, and mammals in one of the prime marine habitats of the world.

CAUSES OF THE WRECK

At one level of analysis, the causes of this accident can be considered to be simple and obvious: An intoxicated captain set the wrong course, and the tanker ran aground on the most clearly charted reef in Prince William Sound, 10 miles south of the proper shipping channel. It is necessary to remember, however, that intoxication has never been proven. Captain Hazelwood admitted that he had been drinking prior to sailing, but he has maintained that he was not drunk, and no witnesses could be found to swear that he was drunk at the time of the accident. It is also necessary to admit that there were numerous other factors *under the control of the company* that contributed both to the grounding of the tanker and to the slowness of the response to the spill.

In this discussion of the accident and the consequences of that accident, I should like to limit the causes to those that could have been corrected by the Exxon Corporation. There was an obvious lack of attention by the Coast Guard, which should have been able to monitor and correct the course of the tanker on its radar, and there was an obvious lack of supervision by the state regulators, who should have insisted that Alyeska Pipeline Service Company be prepared to follow the written agreement on the containment and recovery of oil spills. But in this chapter we are looking at the influence of organizational pressures on the moral decisions of managers, and so I wish to exclude the federal and state agencies. Despite that exclusion in this account, I think that most impartial observers would agree that both the U.S. Coast Guard and the Alaskan Department of Natural Resources bear some of the blame for both the occurrence and the severity of the accident.

What were the factors under the control of the Exxon Corporation that led first to the occurrence and then to the severity of the accident? Let me suggest that they can be divided into three different levels of causation that correspond roughly with three different levels in the management of the company: functional, divisional, and corporate.

Functional and Operating Causes of the Accident

There were a number of unsafe conditions, both on board the ship and at the terminal, that affected the operations at the functional (pumping, loading, and shipping the crude oil) level of the company. Had these unsafe conditions been corrected earlier, they probably would have either prevented the occurrence or ameliorated the severity of the oil spill.

1. *Lack of experience by the third officer.* Mr. Cousins, the third mate, either did not realize the need or have the training to disconnect the automatic steering. The orders he gave to the helmsman were correct, but the ship did not respond. It is felt that a more experienced officer would have recognized the need to disconnect the automatic steering or would have called for emergency steering with the engines when the ship did not respond to the first course correction made with the rudder.

2. *Lack of attention by members of the crew.* Every experienced seaman on board must have known that the tanker was far off course and headed directly toward a submerged reef. It was a clear night. Visibility was over 10 miles. The reef location was known, and marked with a lighted buoy. No one voiced any concern, and the single lookout who was on duty was on the bridge, 1,000 feet back from his proper station at the bow. It is felt that had the lookout been at the bow, or had any seamen on duty been attentive, they would have been able to warn the third officer in time for a much earlier course correction.

3. *Lack of emergency equipment at the shore base.* Two barges to carry the containment booms were specified in the emergency oil spill plan; only one was stationed in Valdez, and it had been damaged in a winter storm nine weeks before the accident. The proper number of booms for containment of the oil spill were not in stock. The proper lengths of hose for transfer of the remaining oil were not available. The emergency lighting system, to help in laying booms and recovering oil at night, could not be found (it had been loaned to a winter carnival). Ten skimmers were available as promised in the plan, but repair parts were not kept in stock, and equipment breakdowns were common as the skimmers were not designed to collect the emulsified mousse mixture of oil and water that had formed through wave action in the noncontained spill. Only 69 gallons of chemical dispersants, to break up the mousse into small droplets that would be much easier to collect with the skimmers, were in the warehouse at Valdez, and 10,000 gallons were needed to treat an oil spill of this size.

4. *Lack of trained personnel at the shore base.* Prior to 1981, there had been a dedicated oil spill response team of 12 persons stationed at Valdez. This team had been disbanded as an unnecessary expense, and its duties had been assigned to the regular employees at the terminal. There had, however, been little training of the regular employees, and consequently there was a delay in loading the long and heavy containment booms on the one remaining barge at the terminal, and there was confusion in unloading, connecting, and positioning these booms at the wreck site. One senior employee said that there had been "zero oil spill training, none" in the years preceding the accident. He said that he had been summoned to a small spill previously and added, "I didn't know what the hell I was supposed to do, and when I found the guy I was supposed to report to, he did not know what the hell we were supposed to do either. We just stood there watching."[3]

Divisional and Budgetary Causes of the Accident

The Exxon Shipping Company is a wholly owned division of Exxon U.S.A., which in turn is one of the five regional companies in the Exxon Corporation. Exxon Shipping is responsible for the operations of all company-owned or company-chartered oil tankers in North America, including the *Exxon Valdez.* The Alyeska Pipeline Service Company is not a wholly owned division of Exxon; instead, it is a consortium, owned jointly by the seven oil companies that have drilling rights on the North Slope of Alaska, near Prudhoe Bay. As explained previously, Alyeska is responsible for the operation of the oil pipeline from Prudhoe Bay to Valdez and for the management of the oil terminal at Valdez. These were the two divisions, responsible for the management of the pumping, loading, and shipping operations. There were a number of conditions at both divisions that contributed to the occurrence and the severity of the oil spill.

1. *Overconfidence by the managers of the two divisions.* Oil had been shipped for 18 years through the pipeline and terminal managed by Alyeska, and on the tankers owned or chartered by Exxon Shipping, without a major spill. Apparently, a general feeling that "It can't happen here" developed among the managers of both companies. Many of the shipboard requirements for the use of experienced officers licensed for navigation in the sea channels approaching Valdez and for the assignment of lookouts on the bow rather than the bridge had gradually become neglected over the years. Many of the shore terminal requirements for the stocking of equipment and the training of personnel had also become gradually ignored over the years. It is probably fair to say that the wreck of the *Exxon Valdez* was an accident waiting to happen.

2. *Lack of funding for the managers of the two divisions.* It is probably also fair to say that the managers of the Exxon Shipping Company and the Alyeska Pipeline Service Corporation were not uncaring, uncommitted people who calmly accepted the inevitability of an accident waiting to happen in Prince William Sound. They were unable to take precautions against that accident because they managed the pumping, loading, and shipping operations under an ongoing shortage of funds and a continual pressure for profits.

Capital allocations for the purchase of new equipment had often been rejected or delayed. At the time of the accident, a new barge had been ordered and built to carry and lay the containment booms; the barge had to have a special hydraulic crane that would adjust to the roughness of the sea in order to properly position the containment booms. However, it was still in Seattle because the funds to pay for it had been appropriated too late for shipment before the winter storms.

Operating budgets for the expenses of both the ships and the terminal had continually been reduced. Exxon tankers had originally sailed with a crew of 45. This crew size had been gradually reduced to 22 officers and crew members over the past five years. The company said that new technologies automated the operation of the large tankers and reduced the need for a larger crew. Crew members said that they were forced to work 15 hours per day while at sea and that they were exhausted and frequently not alert. As a result, it was said, they often took the easier stations, on the bridge and not on the bow, with the permission of the officers who recognized the symptoms of overwork. It is even claimed that Captain Hazelwood left the bridge and returned to his cabin, not because he had been drinking and was tired, but because there was paperwork that had to be done soon after leaving port, and the ship no longer carried a stenographer/clerk who could prepare those reports.

The same large reductions in staff had occurred at the oil terminal. It has already been explained that the dedicated oil spill response team ("dedicated" meant that the 12 members of that team had no other duties than to be prepared to quickly contain and then recover oil spills in the harbor and sea-lanes approaching Valdez) had been disbanded in 1981. The terminal work force generally had been reduced by 50 percent between 1986 and

1989, and personnel able to operate the cranes, barges, and tugs were no longer automatically included on every shift. "There was an overall attitude of petty cheapness that severely affected our ability to operate safely," stated a former manager of the marine operations at the terminal. "I was shocked at the shabbiness of the operations."[4]

Newspaper accounts following the accident supported the allegations of budget shortfalls and insufficient funding. *The Wall Street Journal* reported that one year

> Alyeska managers prepared what they thought was a lean budget and presented it to a meeting of the owners' committee [representatives from the seven major oil companies that jointly owned the consortium] in San Francisco. According to former Alyeska officials who were briefed on the meeting at the time, committee members cited a figure, roughly $220 million, and asked if the budget was under that; told that it wasn't, they rejected the proposed budget out of hand.[5]

Corporate and Strategic Causes of the Accident

I think that it is safe to say that the delays in the capital appropriations and the reductions in the expense budgets were not the result of arbitrary decisions by corporate executives and thoughtless procedures by corporate staff. Instead, they were the result of major changes in the corporate strategy, structure, systems, and style, which in turn were reactions to major alterations in the economic conditions of the worldwide petroleum industry.

The overriding economic condition in the oil industry during the period 1981 to 1989 was the instability in the price of crude oil. Following the shortages of the Arabian Oil Embargo of 1978 and the Iranian Oil Blockade of 1981, the price of crude oil had risen to $32 per barrel, and it was expected to go higher in the years following 1981. Instead, there was an unexpected underusage by Western Europe, the United States, and Japan; an unanticipated overproduction by OPEC members; and a decline in the price of crude oil, to a low of $12 per barrel in 1986. The price had only partially recovered to $18 per barrel by 1989. Companies such as the Exxon Corporation that produced much of their own crude oil rather than purchasing it on the open market had to adjust to much lower profit margins, and they did this by changing the strategy, the structure, the systems, and the style of the firm.

1. *Changes in the corporate strategy.* Exxon deliberately attempted to achieve a low-cost position in the transportation, refining, and distribution of oil products. Senior executives realized that they could not compete with OPEC in the low-cost production of crude oil, and consequently they "restructured" to reduce the "downstream" expenses. Out of a total of 145,000 employees, 45,000 were offered early retirement, and the older, specialized managers and workers who did not accept the offer were forced to resign. No dedicated teams for emergencies such as refinery fires or tanker spills were left in place. No excess staffing for terminals or ships was permitted.

2. *Changes in the organizational structure.* Exxon deliberately "flattened" its structure to create fewer layers between senior managers at the corporate level and operating personnel at the functional level. The fewer layers meant reduced supervision of the divisions by the corporate staff and reduced supervision of operations by the divisional personnel. No longer was an Exxon manager assigned solely to supervise company interests in the Alyeska Pipeline Service Company. Instead, supervision of Alyeska was just one of the responsibilities of the West Coast manager for Exxon U.S.A. Fewer divisional managers were sent to Valdez, and those that were assigned to the oil terminal were responsible for a much wider range of operations. Exxon Shipping suffered from the same reductions in divisional personnel and the same widening of individual responsibilities.

3. *Changes in the managerial systems.* The managerial systems for planning, control, and motivation are interrelated within a company, both conceptually and pragmatically. Strategic planning looks at environmental assumptions, organizational resources, and managerial intentions and then settles upon a long-term strategy or method of competition within an industry. Program planning allocates the resources necessary to implement that strategy. Budgetary planning forecasts the revenues and expenses, and establishes numerical measures of the achievement of the strategy. Operational accounting records the actual results of the achievement in numerical terms, and then comparative evaluation analyzes the variances between the planned outcomes and the actual results. This comparison between planned outcomes and actual results is the basic control system, or evaluation method, that is in use in nearly every major company worldwide. The control system or evaluation method is almost inevitably connected to the motivation system. Performance that meets or exceeds planned outcomes is rewarded by bonuses or by promotions. There is, in well-managed companies, a direct interrelationship between planning, control, and motivation; these interrelationships can be seen graphically in Exhibit 6–2.

At the time of the accident in Prince William Sound, Exxon was a well-managed company. As the strategy and structure of the company shifted, there was a deliberate change in the planning, control, and motivation systems. Planning at the budgetary level began, as has been described, to emphasize cost reductions rather than revenue expansions. Control, which is the comparison of the actual results of operations to the planned outcomes of the budget, also focused on cost reductions. Motivation, which is the award of incentives to the managers whose actual results meet or exceed their planned outcomes, followed in precisely the same pattern.

It was not just that bonuses and promotions tended to follow successful cost reductions in the operations of the pipeline, terminal, and tankers. Executives began to feel that their careers were increasingly at risk due to the forceful downsizing of the firm. One Exxon manager was quoted as saying, "I feel my neck is in the noose. If I don't deliver, they'll get someone in here that will."[6] An Alyeska manager said he was told, "If you can't ship our oil and meet your budget, we'll find somebody else who can."[7]

4. *Changes in the leadership style.* Exxon for years had prided itself on a generous, almost paternalistic, attitude toward its employees. Mr. Clifford Garvin, the chairman of Exxon for nine years prior to the severe downsizing initiated in 1986, had once said, "Exxon hasn't existed 104 years without having developed a lot of strengths. No. 1 is the people who are in this company. We have more than our fair share of good people."[8]

EXHIBIT 6–2 _____

Relationship of Planning, Control and Motivational Systems in Corporate Management

	Strategic planning (method of competition)	Environmental assumptions Organizational resources Managerial intentions Strategic alternatives
Planning System	Program planning (allocation of resources)	Net present value Internal rate of return Cost-benefit analysis Competitive position analysis
	Budgetary planning (projection of results)	Revenue forecasts Expense estimations Numerical measures Descriptive standards
Control System	Operational accounting (recording of performance)	Cost accumulation systems Cost allocation systems Responsibility centers Transfer prices and shared costs
	Comparative evaluation (analysis of variances)	Organizational control Program control Management control Operational control
Motivation System	Organizational response (design of incentives)	Perceptual response Financial response Positional response Personal response
	Individual response (actions and decisions)	Personal influence Interpersonal influence Social influence Cultural influence

SOURCE: LaRue Hosmer, _Strategic Management: Text and Cases on Business Policy_ (Englewood Cliffs, N.J.: Prentice-Hall, 1982), p. 566.

Mr. Lawrence Rawls, who became chairman of Exxon in 1986 and initiated the severe downsizing, had a different attitude toward employees and a different leadership style: "I'm bottom line oriented. I look at the revenues, and then I look at everything that comes in between [that is, the variable costs and fixed expenses]. When I find something that looks a little bit soft, I take a _hard_ look. When the good times are rolling, you can ignore some of that stuff. But, when times get difficult, you've got to do something. In fact, you should do it anyway. That's management. That's what shareholders pay us for."[9]

Assume that you were a manager assigned to the Alyeska Pipeline Service Company in charge of inventory control and storage. You know that there are not enough containment booms in stock to handle a large oil spill. You know that there should be two barges on hand but only one is in the harbor and that one was damaged in a storm nine weeks previously. You can arrange for replacement of the booms or repair of the barge, but either action will take you far over your budget for the year. You know what has happened to other managers at Exxon who went far over their budgets for the year. You are concerned about a possible oil spill and the damaging impact that would have upon the environment, but you are also worried about your career. Do you take action? In retrospect, replacement of the booms, hoses, and dispersants and repair of the barge would have been the "right" thing to do. But do you do the right thing?

Or assume that you are a manager working for Exxon Shipping. You know that the tankers now carry only two officers (the captain and the first mate) who are experienced enough to be licensed to navigate in the sea-lanes approaching the port of Valdez. You know that if one of the tankers happens to leave port late at night, an inexperienced officer will be on the bridge, for it is traditional for the third mate to take the 12:00 midnight to 4:00 A.M. watch, and for the second mate to take the 4:00 A.M. to 8:00 A.M. duty. You also know that it would be much more expensive to hire experienced officers for those positions. You have the authority to make that decision, but do you? Or do you say to yourself, "There hasn't been a major oil spill in Prince William Sound for the past 18 years, and, with any luck, there won't be one for the next three to four years while I am responsible for the staffing of the tankers"?

I think that we can agree that the organizational pressures at Exxon—the strategy, the structure, the systems, and the style—all tended to push managers toward saving money by reducing the number of experienced officers on board the tankers and toward avoiding the capital appropriations and budget expansions necessary to maintain a high state of preparedness at the shore stations. In short, the organizational pressures tended to push managerial decisions and actions strongly toward the economic performance of the firm and definitely away from the social performance of the company.

What could have been done at Exxon to avoid placing managers in this fundamental moral quandary, in which they had to choose between the economic and social performance of the company, between their careers and their responsibilities? Let us start our investigation of this question by assuming that it was not the intent of Lawrence Rawls, chairman of the Exxon Corporation and initiator of the downsizing strategy, to reduce costs at the expense of worker protection (refinery fires) or environmental deterioration (tanker spills). Let us assume that he believed that company managers at the divisional and functional levels would know that it was necessary to maintain safe operating conditions despite the strategy that emphasized cost reduction and capital conservation, and despite the control and motivation systems that both measured and rewarded performance based upon those two dimensions.

Given Mr. Rawls's intention of maintaining safe operating conditions despite the cost reduction and capital conservation goals, how could he have conveyed that expectation to all Exxon employees? He could have simply called a series of meetings and talked to the employees. But there were more than 100,000 employees left even after the restructuring was completed, and these people were spread over the entire globe, for Exxon truly was and is an international firm. The meetings would necessarily have been large, to fit in all of the employees in a reasonable time frame, and large meetings offer no opportunity for questions to be answered and illustrations to be given. He could have simply written a series of letters stressing the need to maintain safe operating conditions. But mass-mailed letters tend not to be read with great care, and an attempt in one or two pages to explain the desired choice between severe cost reductions and safe operating conditions might have confused more than informed the employees.

As an alternative to large meetings or mass mailings, Mr. Rawls could have prepared a written code of ethics to convey his expectations on social versus economic performance; instituted an informal review process to advise on social versus economic performance; or reexamined the strategy, structure, systems, and style of the company to set clear priorities between social and economic performance. Let us look more closely at each of these three alternatives.

WRITTEN CODE OF ETHICS TO CONVEY PERFORMANCE EXPECTATIONS

A written code of ethics is a statement of the norms and beliefs of an organization. It is an attempt to describe "the way we are going to do things around here", with a particular emphasis upon "actions that are simply not acceptable in this organization." A written code of ethics, in brief, is an attempt to set the moral standards of the firm.

The norms and beliefs in a written code of ethics are generally proposed, discussed, and defined by the senior executives in the firm, and then published and distributed to all of its employees. Norms, of course, are standards of behavior; they are the ways the senior people in the organization want the others to act when confronted with a given situation. An example of a norm in a code of ethics would be "Employees of this company will not accept personal gifts with a monetary value over $25 in total from any business friend or associate, and they are expected to pay their full share of the costs for meals or other entertainment (concerts, the theater, sporting events, etc.) that have a value above $25 per person." The norms in an ethical code are generally expressed as a series of negative statements, for it is easier to list the things a person should not do than to be precise about the things a person should do.

The beliefs in an ethical code are standards of thought; they are the ways that the senior people in the organization want others to think when confronted with a given situation. This is not censorship. Instead, the intent is to encourage ways of thinking and patterns of thought that will lead toward the desired behavior. Consequently, the beliefs in an ethical code are generally expressed in a positive form. "Our first responsibility is to our customers" is an example of a positive belief that sometimes appears in codes of ethics; another would be "We wish to be good citizens of every community in which we operate."

Do ethical codes work? Are they helpful in conveying the moral standards selected by the board of directors and president to all others working within the firm? Yes, *provided* those moral standards obviously apply to everyone, not just the personnel at the operating level, *and provided* the board of directors and president make an effort to address the moral problems actually faced by employees at the divisional and operating levels.

Many written codes of ethics are just detailed explanations of corporate expectations relative to financial honesty and legal scrupulousness. Look at the summary statements in the code of ethics of Exxon U.S.A., the regional portion of Exxon Corporation responsible directly for Exxon Shipping Company and indirectly for Alyeska Pipeline Service Company (Exhibit 6–3). The statements can be further summarized as "Be honest, be truthful, obey the law, and avoid conflicts of interest." There is certainly nothing wrong with honesty, truthfulness, legality, and the avoidance of conflicts of interest, but I assume that many readers are at least

EXHIBIT 6–3 _____

Summary Code of Ethics of Exxon Company, U.S.A.

Business Ethics

Our company policy is one of strict observance of all laws applicable to its business.

A reputation for scrupulous dealing is itself a priceless Company asset.

We do care how we get results.

We expect candor at all levels and compliance with accounting rules and controls.

Antitrust

It is the established policy of the Company to conduct its business in compliance with all state and federal antitrust laws.

Individual employees are responsible for seeing that they comply with the law.

Employees must avoid even the appearance of violation.

Conflict of Interest

Competing or conducting business with the Company is not permitted, except with the knowledge and consent of management.

Accepting and providing gifts, entertainment, and services must comply with specific requirements.

An employee may not use Company personnel, information, or other assets for personal benefit.

Participating in certain outside activities requires the prior approval of management.

SOURCE: Exxon Company, U.S.A. Company document, December 1988.

mildly troubled by the apparent direction of the statements toward the lower levels of the firm (There is a list of actions that cannot be undertaken except with the prior approval of management; who approves equivalent actions by those managers?), and by the obvious exclusion from the statements of any expressed concern for worker safety, environmental pollution, customer service, or distributor loyalty.

Now, look at the written code of ethics of Johnson & Johnson, the large drug company and distributor of medical supplies (Exhibit 6–4). There is no mention of financial honesty or legal adherence. Perhaps those virtues are assumed. Instead there is an explicit listing, in an obvious order of priority, of the accepted social responsibilities of the firm. You are certainly welcome to disagree, but I would like to say that I think that the Credo of Johnson & Johnson is an impressive document.

Do they mean it? Are the senior executives at Johnson & Johnson actually willing to place the welfare of their customers, employees, and communities above the profits of their stockholders? Apparently they are, or at least apparently they were at the time of the Tylenol scare in 1982. The company spent over $100 million removing Tylenol (a nonprescription drug that was found to have been deliberately poisoned in Chicago, causing the deaths of four individuals) from the shelves of every store within the United States. Mr. James Burke, chairman of Johnson & Johnson, credits the written code of ethics with guiding the actions of his company.

> This document spells out our responsibilities to all of our constituencies: consumers, employees, community and stockholders. It served to guide all of us during the crisis, when hard decisions had to be made in what were often excruciatingly brief periods of time. All of our employees worldwide were able to watch the process of the Tylenol withdrawal and subsequent reintroduction in tamper-resistant packaging, confident of the way in which the decisions would be made. There was a great sense of shared pride in the knowledge that the Credo was being tested . . . and it worked![10]

It is difficult to state the norms and beliefs of an organization relative to the various constituent groups—employees, customers, suppliers, distributors, stockholders, and the general public—clearly and explicitly. Most companies cannot do this in a written code of ethics because they have not thought through, as part of

EXHIBIT 6–4 _____

Code of Ethics of Johnson & Johnson, Inc.

_____

Our Credo

We believe our first responsibility is to the doctors, nurses and patients, to mothers and all others who use our products and services.

In meeting their needs everything we do must be of high quality.

We must constantly strive to reduce our costs in order to maintain reasonable prices.

Customers' orders must be serviced promptly and accurately.

Our suppliers and distributors must have an opportunity to make a fair profit.

We are responsible to our employees, the men and women who work with us throughout the world.

Everyone must be considered as an individual.

We must respect their dignity and recognize their merit.

They must have a sense of security in their jobs.

Compensation must be fair and adequate, and working conditions clean, orderly and safe.

Employees must feel free to make suggestions and complaints.

There must be equal opportunity for employment, development and advancement for those qualified.

We must provide competent management, and their actions must be just and ethical.

We are responsible to the communities in which we live and work and to the world community as well.

We must be good citizens—support good works and charities and bear our fair share of taxes.

We must encourage civic improvements and better health and education.

We must maintain in good order the property we are privileged to use, protecting the environment and natural resources.

Our final responsibility is to our stockholders.

Business must make a sound profit.

We must experiment with new ideas.

Research must be carried on, innovative programs developed and mistakes paid for.

New equipment must be purchased, new facilities provided and new products launched.

Reserves must be created to provide for adverse times.

When we operate according to these principles, the stockholders should realize a fair return.

SOURCE: Johnson & Johnson, Inc. Company annual report for 1982, p. 5.

their strategy, structure, and systems exactly what are those norms and beliefs. I think that we can conclude that written codes of ethics can be effective in guiding the decisions and actions of managers at the divisional and functions levels *provided* the statements clearly reflect the expectations of the senior executives relative to the social performance of the firm in an orderly, prioritized listing, *and provided* it is accepted that those expectations relative to social performance will be maintained despite an adverse impact upon the financial performance of the firm.

INFORMAL REVIEW PROCESS TO ADVISE ON PERFORMANCE EXPECTATIONS

Some companies have set up an informal review process to counsel managers at the divisional and operating levels on ethical problems that involve a conflict between the economic and social performance of the firm. The feeling is that executives in the formal review process, that is, executives at a higher level in the structural hierarchy of the firm, are subject to the same organizational pressures as are their subordinates, and consequently they are unable to properly advise subordinates. Think for a minute about being the head of the Exxon Shipping Company, given the corporate emphasis upon cost reductions. Would you really want one of your subordinates asking you what to do about the use of inexperienced officers directing oil tankers in and out of the port of Valdez? This is not a very generous view of the process of management, but it is said that many divisional managers in large companies would prefer not to know what can go wrong within their divisions. If you don't know, the reasoning is, you can't really be blamed when something does go wrong. If you do know, then you probably will have to take some action, and that action may not be very popular with the senior executives at the corporate level. It is easy for you to convey to your own subordinates the attitude that you don't want to be bothered with operating details and that they will have to settle such issues following their own initiative.

As another example, think for a minute about being the head of the Alyeska Pipeline Service Company. Would you really want your subordinates asking you what to do about the shortages of emergency supplies and trained personnel? Again, you might be tempted to tell them that the details of inventory levels and training schedules are their concerns, not yours. You might be worried that your own career would be at risk if you tried to push through the capital appropriations and budget increases necessary to remedy those shortages.

An informal review process provides an indirect, nonthreatening means of obtaining a response from senior management on a conflict between economic and social performance. An ombudsman is appointed. This is a person within an organization, often an older and respected manager who is close to retirement and who has been relieved of operating responsibilities and assigned the task of counseling younger employees on career issues, organizational difficulties, and moral problems. The term is Swedish; it originally referred to a government agent in that country who had been especially appointed to investigate complaints made by individual citizens against public officials for abuses of power or unfeeling, uncaring acts. Often the ombudsman, whether in a business firm or public office, can go considerably beyond counseling and investigation and is able to act informally to resolve moral problems. As an example, we can consider the case of the manager mentioned in the first chapter who was attempting to force all of the employees working for him to use his frequent flyer card while traveling on company business so that he could accumulate the free trips and vacation discounts. Were there an ombudsman in that company, the recent graduate of a business school who reported the practice to me could have reported it to the ombudsman. That person could than have counseled the recent graduate either by saying, "Forget it; lots of people do that around here," or (and let us hope this would be the reaction) the ombudsman could have told her, "You do not need to be concerned any longer; I will take care of the matter and see that this is stopped, without implicating you in any way." Then the ombudsman could have met informally with the manager responsible and told him that the practice was totally unacceptable. An older and respected member of a firm, close to retirement yet also close to the president and members of the board, can correct many improper situations informally, without concern about later retribution.

Does the informal review process symbolized by the ombudsman really work? Again, yes, but only if the person occupying that position is truly clear in his or her own mind on the priorities of the senior executives of the firm. The priorities of the senior executives on questions of economic versus social performance are the true values of the firm. As with written codes of ethics, many times these values have never been explicitly stated or, even better, obviously followed by the senior executives. The ombudsman can help in bringing moral problems to their attention and in asking for clarification, but the person holding that position cannot, by himself or herself, resolve those conflicts between economic and social performance.

REEXAMINATION OF THE STRATEGY, STRUCTURE, SYSTEMS AND STYLE

Written codes of ethics and informal review processes are seldom as effective as might be desired in resolving the conflicts that exist within most companies between the economic and the social performance of the firm. The priorities between economic and social performance are the true values of the firm, but most companies have not thought through—as part of their strategy, structure, systems, and style—exactly what those values are.

It is the argument of this book that senior executives have a responsibility to "think through" the priorities of the firm relative to the conflict between economic and social performance, rather than pushing decisions on those conflicts down to the lower portions of the organization. It is the argument of this book that senior executives have a responsibility to set the values of the firm clearly for employees at the functional and divisional levels so that the employees know exactly what is expected of them when they encounter moral dilemmas.

How do senior managers think through these conflicts and set those values? They should start with strategic planning and recognize the effect of alternative strategies upon each of the constituent groups within the organization. "We can increase profits substantially by eliminating the dedicated teams for refinery fires and oil spills at each of our facilities, but what will be the impact of that staffing change upon the safety of our employees and the quality of our environment?" It should have been reasonably clear at the time that the cost-reduction strategy was first being considered that such a staffing change could have a very adverse impact upon employee safety and environmental quality, even given the low probability of accidents derived from past data. After all, accidents do happen, and the company as part of its strategic planning process should have prepared for the eventuality of an accident. "We recognize that the elimination of the dedicated teams could have an adverse impact upon worker saftey and environmental quality, and consequently we will provide meaningful response training for all of our personnel and we will maintain complete emergency supplies at all of our facilities."

Then it is necessary for senior executives, as part of program planning (for resource allocations) and budgetary planning (for revenue and expense projections), to ensure that capital is provided for the emergency supplies and that expenses are included for the response training. Next, the control system has to be changed to reflect the altered priorities. It is not enough to simply ask the manager of the oil terminal at Valdez, "Did you meet our revenue and expense projections?" As part of that person's annual review it is necessary to add a number of additional questions: "Is our stock of the emergency supplies needed to contain a major oil spill complete?" "Are the two barges listed in our emergency plan fully maintained and ready for service?" "Are our employees thoroughly trained to respond to a major oil spill, and what was the response time at the most recent training exercise?"

Finally, the motivation system has to be changed to reflect the different controls. If a bonus is to be paid for keeping within revenue and expense projections, then a bonus should also be paid for maintaining the essential supplies, repairing the emergency equipment, and meeting the response times needed to mitigate an environmental disaster. If that second bonus is not included in the motivation system, it sends a message throughout the organization that the mitigation of environmental disasters is not nearly as important as the improvement of corporate profits.

Thinking through the obligations of the firm toward its different constituencies (customers, employees, owners, etc.) and setting the values of the firm on its various conflicts between economic and social outcomes are not easy tasks. It is hard to recognize all the obligations and anticipate all the conflicts, but it is even more difficult to know exactly what to do about them. We saw in the last chapter, on the moral choice of individuals, that there are no completely satisfactory means of reaching a decision when confronted by an ethical dilemma. We have to conclude in this chapter, on the moral design of organizations, that there are no completely satisfactory means of setting a strategy when confronted with obligations to different groups and conflicts between different outcomes. Multiple analysis—using economic, legal, and moral forms of reasoning—does appear to clarify the issues and does seem to generate solutions that can be considered to be more "right", more "just", and more "fair" than solutions that do not make use of the multiple forms of analysis, but that process of analysis does not guarantee either unanimity or certainty. It does not guarantee unanimity because the values—the priorities between economic, legal, and moral outcomes—are bound to differ among members of the organization. It does not guarantee certainty because the probabilities—the chances of those outcomes actually occurring—are bound to be unknown.

What were the probabilities of the *Exxon Valdez* actually running aground on Bligh Reef, 10 miles south of the proper course through Prince William Sound? Prior to the accident, those probabilities could not have been calculated. Could the senior management at Exxon have agreed upon the "proper" level of preparation for that potential accident? Probably not. Yet business firms must be managed with the recognition that they do have obligations to a wide range of constituencies and that they will encounter conflicts between economic and social outcomes. How can this be done?

THE MORAL RESPONSIBILITIES OF SENIOR MANAGEMENT

In most companies, under current conditions, the obligations to different constituencies and the conflicts between different outcomes are simply ignored by senior management. The attitude generally is that those obligations and conflicts are "operating problems"—after all, they deal with such issues as hiring experienced versus inexperienced second and third officers for the tankers or scheduling crane operators for all shifts at the terminals—and they are pushed down to the divisional and functional levels. The problem is that at those levels most conflicts between economic and social outcomes will be settled in favor of the economic side of the balance. Why? Because under existing managerial systems, the performance of those managers is measured by economic criteria, and their future is dependent upon economic results.

The obligations to the different constituencies and the conflicts among the different outcomes must be addressed and resolved at the senior level, as part of the strategic planning process.

Senior managers must recognize the potential impacts of the alternative strategies upon the different constituencies of the firm. Senior managers must anticipate the potential conflicts within the alternative strategies of the economic and social performance levels of the firm. And they have to decide, and then convey that decision to others.

How can this be done, given the lack of certainty and the lack of unanimity that are inherent in the strategic planning process? My response is *with character and courage.* This is the character to face the obligations and conflicts—not to sidestep or avoid them—and the courage to thoughtfully evaluate each of the alternatives and then arrive at a solution. This is the character to recognize moral problems and the courage to express ethical decisions.

Others may disagree with the ethical decision of an executive because of differences in their perspectives within the firm or because of differences in their beliefs in the importance of the economic outcomes, the legal requirements, the moral principles of beneficiency and consistency, or the moral values of justice and liberty. We have a multitude of economic, legal, and ethical outcomes, requirements, principles, and values, but no clear ordering between them. This is not an excuse, however, to avoid making ethical decisions in management. We have to make those decisions based upon our sense of responsibility to others; it is a test of our character and a measure of our courage.

Notes

1. *The Wall Street Journal,* March 31, 1989, p.1.
2. Ibid.
3. *The Wall Street Journal,* July 6, 1989, p.1.
4. Ibid.
5. Ibid.
6. *Business Week,* July 15, 1988, p. 107.
7. Statement of oil industry executive, made in confidence to the author.
8. *Fortune,* January 6, 1986, p. 20.
9. *Fortune,* April 14, 1986, p. 27.
10. Annual Report of Johnson & Johnson, 1982, p. 2.

CASES

Three Companies in Need of Moral Direction

The three short cases following Chapter 5 depicted moral problems encountered by recent graduates of a program in business administration. These were fundamental moral problems, for in each instance they placed the career of the individual in jeopardy if he or she refused to accept the situation. The recent graduates had to decide what they would or would not accept; they had to decide where they would draw the line.

Now, you have been promoted. Put yourself in the place of the president of one of those companies (or the managing partner in the instance of the accounting firm). Just to help your memory, the moral problems involved (1) a plant manager for a metal stamping company who was accepting kickbacks from a steel supplier, (2) an office manager for an accounting firm who was trying to conceal evidence of financial wrongdoing by a client, and (3) a production process at a chemical plant that was tolerated by the plant manager even though it was harmful to the health and well-being of the employees.

You are president or partner or clearly at a managerial level where you can make whatever decision you believe would serve the best interests of your company and your society. You also have a reputation as a "tough guy"—a man or woman who has managed the company very successfully in the past (continually increasing sales and profits) and consequently a person who tends to get his or her own way in dealing with stockholders, board members, and subordinates so that you know that it will be possible to implement whatever decision you make. That decision may or may not accomplish what you want, but at least people in your company will try to make it work.

Finally, you have just found that the situation described in the case actually exists in your firm and, even worse, you have hard evidence that it is endemic throughout the firm. That is, if you decided to be president of the metal stamping company, you have irrefutable evidence that numerous people throughout the company are accepting small kickbacks. If instead you put yourself in the place of the president of the chemical company, you now understand that almost all of your chemical plants have at least one production process that is technically legal but medically and environmentally harmful. You are shocked. You say to your spouse that night, "I had no idea this was going on, but it obviously is, and I've got to do something about it."

Class Assignment.   What exactly do you do? You can fire the people involved, but will that really cure the problem? What other actions can you take that will "cure the problem"?

Code of Ethics for a School of Business Administration

Your school may or may not have a formal code of ethics or a written code of conduct. The two are basically the same; only the terms in the title seem to differ, as well as some degree of emphasis upon what is "right" (ethics) or what is "permitted" (conduct).

If your school does have such a code, it probably focuses primarily upon the actions of the students. Most do. However, a school of business administration within a college or university has a much wider range of constituent groups. One way of looking at such a school (stakeholder analysis) is that it actually consists of the internal faculty, staff, and students, and the external alumni who offer support, companies that employ graduates, foundations that provide gifts, firms that supply services, and so forth.

Class Assignment.   Put together the outline of a code of ethics or a code of conduct for your school. It is suggested that you start by looking at the two codes that are published in Chapter 6. The code of the Exxon Corporation tends to be negative; it lists a series of the actions that are prohibited. The code of Johnson & Johnson tends to be positive; it lists a series of duties toward each of the constituent groups. Decide which type you prefer, and then try to include most of the constituent groups in your outline.

1. The code of ethics (Credo) of Johnson & Johnson puts the customers in the first place. If you selected a positive type of code, similar to the Credo, which group do you place first?
2. The code of ethics of the Exxon Corporation specifically prohibits a series of actions by employees. If you selected a negative type of code, what actions do you prohibit?
3. If you are pleased with the final content, structure, and wording of your proposed code, think about the problems of implementation. If published, would it be followed?

The Shortest Case in any BBA or MBA Program

Clarence Walton, formerly dean of the College of General Studies at Columbia and president of the Catholic College of America, provides a very different concept of leadership in the first chapter of his recent book, *The Moral Manager*:

> Leadership, an ill-defined word, comes from understanding and respecting four crucial ideas: equality, justice, truth and freedom.[1]

Class Assignment.

1. Do you agree with Professor Walton? Why or why not?
2. If you do agree with Professor Walton, why do almost all programs in business administration spend so much time on accounting, statistics, computers, marketing, production, and finance, and so little on "equality, justice, truth and freedom"?
3. If you don't agree with Professor Walton, what "four crucial ideas" would you substitute? List them below.

First crucial idea: _____

Second crucial idea: _____

Third crucial idea: _____

Fourth crucial idea: _____

Note

1. Clarence Walton, *The Moral Manager* (Cambridge, Mass.: Ballinger Publishing Company, 1988), p. 4.

Subject Index